HUMAN RIGHTS, CRIMES AGAINST HUMANITY AND STATE TERROR

M. ABDULLAH ZAKIR

**Published by
Zap-Critique Books
5 Sutton Road
Leicester LE2 6FL
United Kingdom
Email: zap.critique@ntlworld.com**

Price in the UK £7.95

Copyright © 2003 M. Abdullah ZAKIR.

The right of M. Abdullah ZAKIR to be identified as the author of this work has been asserted by him under the provisions of the UK Copyright, Designs and Patents Act 1988.

All rights reserved. Except for brief quotations in a review, this book, or any part thereof, must not be reproduced in any form without prior written permission from the publishers.

A cataloguing-in-Publication Data entry for this title is available from the British Library.

ISBN 0-9528889-5-5

First published in Great Britain in 2003 by:
Zap-Critique Books,
5 Sutton Road,
LEICESTER,
LE2 6FL.

Email: zap.critique@ntlworld.com

TABLE OF CONTENTS

		Page No.
Introduction		4

CHAPTER

1	Double Standards and Weapons of Mass Distortion	9
2	Iraq between Two Human Rights Disasters	22
3	The Sedition of Glorifying the Tyrants and Oppressors	37
4	Arab and Muslim Peoples - Victims of Internal Intrigues	54
5	Human Rights and Human Wrongs	72
6	Children – The Silent Victims of Crimes against Humanity	85
7	Instruments of Crime – Lethal Weapons, Small Arms and Nuclear Proliferation	96
8	Torture and War Crimes	107
9	Genocides – Heinous Crimes against Humanity	119
10	Banking on the Ghastly Crime of September 11	137
11	The Crime of Indiscriminate Killings and Reaction of the Biased Media	155
	Conclusion	177
	References	185

INTRODUCTION

THE peace movements, anti-war movements and non-governmental organizations are rendering worthwhile services in defence of human rights under the ambit of their specialization. The deliberations in this study take a broad outlook and encompass a number of burning issues in relation to human rights violations in the modern world.

The agony and sufferings of humankind, whether at family level, or communal, national and international levels, are attributable to oppression and injustice. The resultant condition cannot be improved and remedied until responsibility is pinpointed. Oppression and injustice have no race, no colour and no nationality. Yet, they have perforated every race, every colour and every nation. Their effects, which are bitter and poisonous, are manifested in hatred and resentment that leave deep scars on the physique and psyche of the oppressed. Violence generates violence. Hatred breeds hatred. The vicious cycle continues unabated as humankind pursues a self-destructive course.

If humankind is to be saved from the fatal effects of oppression and injustice, then selfless commitment is required from conscientious men and women of all races, colours, nations and religions. They have to face the challenge of the rising tide of human rights abuses, imposed on the world community, more often than not, by the self-centred politicians. On the basis of political power and might, these politicians have given themselves an almighty right to decide our future, to drag us into unwanted wars, to impose on our fellow human beings artificial starvation, and to spend only an infinitesimal proportion of defence budgets on alleviating world poverty.

As Iraq is dominating the world news and views, human rights violations in that country have been analyzed from different perspectives in this study. Apathetic attitudes in the Arab and Muslim world towards human rights infringements in their own countries and the role of the court-clerics in this transgression have been critically assessed. Rights and wrongs in the modern parlance, the role of international covenants and the United Nations Charter of Human Rights, in successfully theorizing, but failing to have impact in practice, have been argued. Spotlight on the challenges facing the global community on the arms race, poverty, education, abuse of the rights of the children, are covered generally. The inquiry is also focused on the specific areas of war crimes, torture, indiscriminate killings, massacres, ethnic cleansing and genocides.

Post-September 11 events have unmasked the intent and philosophy of power politics. In the process, a number of crucial issues have been muddled by tampering with the human rights of indigenous people. Palestine, Afghanistan, Iraq, Iran, Syria and Lebanon face the far-sighted strategic planning of the think-tank in Washington. The language being promoted is, might is right. The usurpation of the rights of the natives is leading towards an active political volcano that may drag several nations into its lava. Human duties towards the defenceless are being sacrificed at the altar of the superiority syndrome which is shaping the new world order. Survival of the strong and subjugation of the weak is becoming a tangible factor on which, the new global order is being formed, unchallenged by any rival power.

The Middle Eastern countries are likely to remain under surveillance in the foreseeable future. Their guilt is that they are sitting on huge reservoirs of black gold, which is badly needed by the industries in the West. Another significant feature underlying the turmoil is that the US dollar was the only currency of settlement of oil revenues. The Euro has begun to threaten the dollar monopoly. Iraq had already declared that it would accept the settlement of oil contracts in the Euros. Iran also signalled that it would follow suit. If the US dollar was to be replaced by the Euro, and if other oil-producing countries were to follow the trend, this could prove to be more damaging than any weapon of mass destruction.

The Palestinian crisis that threatens world peace should have warranted direct intervention by the United Nations peace-keeping forces to protect the civilians from atrocities. Instead, the tragic plight of the native people had been and is being dehumanized. This discourse illustrates how the human rights of people under occupation are being usurped, in direct breach of international law and the UN Charters and Geneva Convention. If the global community had the courage to honour its own conventions and decisions and adopt a resolute stance against arrogance and pride in world politics, then the world would have been a peaceful place to live in. The root-cause of all the upheaval, turmoil, violence and terror, is oppression and injustice of the strong against the weak, as is amply demonstrated in this study.

Whenever the American and British leaders pay lip-service, in a cursory way, to a future independent Palestinian State, they give the impression that they have said too much. Therefore, immediately thereafter, the next sentence or so has to mention the security of Israel. In his historic address to both Houses of Congress in Washington on 17 July 2003, Prime Minister Tony Blair made a strong point that the security of Israel must never be compromised. This would have been quite a cogent and convincing point had it been the Palestinians and not the Israelis who were occupying other people's territory, attacking the Israeli civilians with helicopter gunships, bulldozing Israeli homes and engaging in extrajudicial killings of the Israeli leaders, without the least regard for any law or human standards.

There is no clause in the UN Charters or international law or Geneva Convention, or even under Western laws that permits the construction of an apartheid wall, worse than the Berlin wall, on forcibly confiscated land. But under the pretext of the 'security of Israel', the West has blessed and in many cases, encouraged the violations of international conventions and international law by successive Israeli governments. In the name of the 'security of Israel' the powerful nations have tolerated massacres of unarmed Palestinian civilians.

Almost three times as many Palestinians have been killed as Israelis in the last half a century, yet, it is always the 'security of Israel' that is at risk. The top officials in the American government are on record as having proudly taken credit that the war on Iraq was

Introduction

also for the sake of 'security of Israel'. Immediately after the war on Iraq, as Ariel Sharon had visualized and declared, the United States directed its threats against Iran, Syria and Lebanon, for the 'security of Israel'.

Another interesting point that Prime Minister Blair made in his speech to the Congress was the need to combat hatred against the Jews. The Prime Minister had only to refer to dozens of websites on the internet where the extremist and fundamentalist Jews and Christians nakedly preach their venom and hatred against the Arabs and Muslims. Some of the fanatical radicals among them even believe that the increasing population of Muslims in the United States is a threat to the 'security of Israel'.

The rights of the Arabs are being written off by applying two different standards of treating ethnic communities in the region. Most of Sharon's victims have to be either 'terrorists' or 'suspected militants'! No trial is needed. No proof is needed. No conviction is needed. Once killed, their corpses provide enough justification for Israeli action. All this is permissible because Israel is the only 'democracy' in the Middle East.

In March and April 2003, foreign correspondents and human rights activists were targeted in an attempt to drive them away from exposing Israeli repression. Several of them were shot at close range. On Channel 4 News on 9 May 2003, Jack Straw, the Foreign and Commonwealth Secretary was asked whether the British government was doing anything about the shooting of the reporters. In answer, he boasted that the Israeli government had volunteered to carry out an inquiry. The internal Israeli inquiry was bound to acquit every high-handed action taken by its troopers, and pronounce them as necessary for the 'security of Israel'.

Sharon's government took the incident of the killing of reporters as a pretext to ban all foreign reporters and human rights activists from entering Gaza. The objective was to circumvent adverse media coverage given to the blowing up of houses. Yet, Sharon has not fully appreciated the esteem and honour he enjoys at the White House. If only he had cared to accept the American 'road map' as it was, without any reservations, he would have been on his

Introduction

way to being nominated for the Nobel Peace Prize, which he could then have shared with his Defence Minister Mofaz, the architect of the massacre in Jenin. The latest orgy of Sharon's assassination of the Hamas leaders has attracted criticism of Shimon Peres and Colin Powell. But then Sharon is confident that the US is not in the mood of putting any pressure on him.

One does not have to be a believer in conspiracy theory in order to perceive and discern the dangerous plots being laid down for the region. The Zion-neoconservative members of the think-tank, whose advice is earnestly sought by influential figures in Washington, do not make a secret of their colonialist aims. One of the most enlightening, well researched and highly readable articles on the web covering this subject is that of Scott Thompson in the *Executive Intelligence Review*.[1]

Some of the kinky ideas boiling up in the think-thank have not even spared the closest ally of the United States - Saudi Arabia. They want the US to control the oil-rich region in Eastern Saudi Arabia. To expect them to spare Iran is implausible. They take pride in getting $50 million allocated to destabilize Iran through internal disturbances. This of course is not terrorism in the dictionary of the think-tank. On the subject of the provoked disturbances in Iran, Lyndon La Rouche said in Istanbul on 14 June 2003: "That is not a spontaneous student movement. This is a U.S.-run destabilization of Iran, trying to set up the conditions for a war. ...We are now inside World War III..."[2]

This study also explores and evaluates the internal factors that are leading the Arabs and Muslims astray on human rights issues. Some nations cannot wash off their hands from responsibility for the turmoil on the international arena. The hypocrisy prevailing in the official circles has contributed to the tumultuous events, which lead to crime and corruption. Corruption results in chaos, which opens a world of opportunity for those who thrive in chaos.

1

Double Standards and Weapons of Mass Distortion

THE age of scientific and technological revolution has abridged national boundaries to make the world a global village. There has been phenomenal development in Information Technology. Multimedia and cyberspace have progressed at a speed that leaves the Industrial Revolution a forgotten past. Humankind has witnessed the mysteries of space exploration and has explored the seabed to discover the amazing existence of other species. Commensurate with the pace of development, new techniques and scientific methods have been invented to destroy human life. The world's helpless and poor are in the forefront to bear the brunt, as if they are the 'untouchable caste' of humankind.

Exuberance in the construction industry has culminated in the towering structures that touch the edge of clouds, but nevertheless carry a blurred view of the state of affairs on the ground. In this age and time, when the developed world cannot even imagine what life would be like without hygienic clean drinking water and electricity, some parts of the world are yet to enjoy these 'luxuries'. The poor and destitute of the world live by the light of candles and kerosene lamps and have access only to polluted drinking water, as if these amenities are an exclusive privilege of the 'chosen caste' of humankind. Only a day's total black-out in eastern United States and Canada created havoc, resulting in multi-million dollar losses. Whereas such black-outs are a daily occurrence in the poor countries.

Governments that are not capable enough of providing the basic necessities of life to their own nationals are more than capable of spending millions on stockpiling heavy arms and arsenal. These governments have already ransomed several generations of their nation by investing scarce resources in arms and ammunitions. They abuse the human rights of their own people for personal, tribal and dynastic dominance.

In the last fifty years, the continents of Asia and Africa have been torn apart by civil wars. The home-grown dictators, with the support of one world power or another, have wasted and splurged the wealth of their nation on weaponry for no other reason than to fight each other. It is not that the policy-makers are ignorant or illiterate. They are normally educated and well trained in the civilized West.

Arms contracts are an easy prey for the totalitarian regimes in the 'Third World' and elsewhere to enrich themselves, their family members and their friends by earning hefty commissions. Some of them do survive to witness their own downfall and disgrace and others leave the menace as a legacy for posterity. Five members of the Security Council manufacture and supply over 90 percent of the world's arms. Therefore, boisterous claims emanating from these countries in the name of 'freedom' and 'democracy' are viewed in the 'Third World' with scepticism.

In the scramble for arms, several scenarios emerge. Manufacturers, who are able to attract heavy investments, are keen to keep the industry buoyant. Their objective cannot be realized if there is no market for deadly weapons. Investments of billions of dollars cannot be seen to dwindle to the point of erosion of capital as this may cause strangleholds in the national economy. Therefore, manufacturers of weapons, with their majority shareholders sitting in the seats of political power, are prone to preach that no moral issues should dictate their policy of supply. It is in their best interest to create new markets around the globe, test the effectiveness of new products on the battlefields, and find the means of disposing of their obsolete lethal stocks.

From the viewpoint of the recipients too, arms have to be brought into use rather than be left to rust in the vagaries of harsh weather conditions. Deadly weapons are supplied in the form of foreign aid, commercial deals or on the black market, depending on how desperate the situation is. Political interest and prospects of profiteering are the main determining factors. The suppliers are assured of guaranteed ongoing demand from unrepresentative and

Chapter 1: Double Standards and Weapons of Mass Distortion

autocratic regimes that face the constant fear of an uprising from their own people.

When these weapons fall into the wrong hands, they nurture an unjust political system. This situation has been responsible for the cruelty and suffering of the people around the globe during the last century. Discords and disputes are instigated and proxies are appointed to fuel the fire of war. The market booms when unscrupulous suppliers end up supplying weapons to both the warring factions, as in the present civil war in Liberia, and enjoy the scenes on their TV screens while the world of the poor and oppressed people is in flames.

Human life is being slowly but surely destroyed with conventional weapons. In the 'Third World' countries, ethnic cleansing, war crimes and genocides have recurred with the perpetual use of these weapons. Charley Reese has posted a very interesting article on the web[3] in which he illustrates how the United States has supported, befriended and financed genocidal tyrannical dictators in modern history. Even as it has declared that its aim is to fight international terrorism, most of these terrorists are the products of its own making and nurturing. They were armed, trained and financed by the CIA.

Eisenhower, the late President of the United States has said: "Every gun that is made, every warship launched, every rocket fired signifies in the final sense, a theft from those who hunger and are not fed, those who are cold and are not clothed. This world in arms is not spending money alone. It is spending the sweat of its laborers, the genius of its scientists, the hopes of its children. This is not a way of life at all in any true sense. Under the clouds of war, it is humanity hanging on a cross of iron."[4]

The latter years were to prove that it was humanity as a whole that was persecuted through arms deals, as envisaged by President Eisenhower. But his appeal fell on deaf ears. The end of the Cold War was not seen as a blessing in disguise, but rather a curse for arms producers. The demand for arms slumped. After almost half a century, nations felt a breeze of tranquillity, but arms manufacturers started suffering from insomnia. Hence, the lobbyists started pressurizing the politicians. New markets had to be explored and the focus had to shift to the developing countries, especially the Middle East. In the words of President Clinton, "...our share of Global Conventional Arms agreements rose from 17 percent in 1988 to 70 percent in 1993..."[5] He said that "unelected governments" were interested in placing large orders "to ensure stability". President Clinton promised the "spectacular growth" of arms contracts and his Administration started working meticulously towards that goal.

In the Bush Administration, a number of economic factors synthesized to produce a scenario, which paved the way to a staggering expansion of the arms industry. As the national economy of the United States dragged the global economy into recession; as the decline in the demand for goods forced the manufacturers to wind up their businesses; as the stock markets dived deep into the murky waters; and as the politicians faced the prospects of being brought to book for their badly failed domestic policies; hence, refuge was sought in reviving the market for the heavy arms industry.

In this way, politicians are able to plan their strategy for the next presidential election. The election donors and financiers are to be kept happy and contented with triple digit percentage profits on sophisticated weaponry in a lucrative market. After the war, rebuilding also is necessary. This has to be paid for liberally from the resources of the country under occupation. With two major wars to his credit, President George W. Bush would face the 'electoral college' this time, not with right punches in wrong holes, but with wrong punches in wrong holes. In the olden times, 'electoral college' was the title enjoyed by the princes and archbishops of the German empire who had exclusive right to elect the emperor. Names have changed but the ideology is the same. Bush would face the electors with a hubristic record of war on Afghanistan and Iraq and with a predictable commitment of armed conflicts in the next presidential term on Lebanon, Syria and Iran. This is what the neoconservative hawks expect of him and on this basis, his election campaign would be financed.

If human rights still carry the same meaning as they carried when the United Nations Charter of Human Rights was passed in

Chapter 1: Double Standards and Weapons of Mass Distortion

1948, then it goes without saying that by occupying other countries, the occupiers are in flagrant violation of the human rights of the occupied people. Human beings are born to live in freedom according to their own will and values. In as much as George Washington abhorred seeing America being occupied by external forces, other nations too have the right of self-determination, to live on their own land in peace and to elect their own rulers and governments.

Behind the slogan of 'weapons of mass destruction', the powerful nations have embarked upon a long-term enterprise, the end result of which, to say the least, is obscure. The US defiantly displayed double standards when it flexed its military muscle under the pretext of enforcing the UN resolution to disarm Iraq. Ironically, the US has obstructed every UN resolution on Israel from being implemented despite that country's record of human rights violations against the occupied people. For decades, Israel has used weapons of mass distortion as a smokescreen to divert the attention of the global community away from its own destructive nuclear capabilities.

No nation in the 'Third World' could possibly embark upon a programme of producing a nuclear bomb without the active involvement of the big nations. The United States played a dominant role in triggering the nuclear race in the Middle East by arming Israel to the teeth with weapons of mass destruction. It compelled other nations in the area to rethink their own defence strategy. Israel became the largest nuclear power in the area. Judging by the brutality of its occupation history, it could easily hold the entire Middle East to ransom.

The powerful nations have held the human rights of developing countries hostage to their own political and economic expediencies. It seems that the idol of 'self-interest' is replacing other deities as an object of worship in modern geopolitics. Injustices in society are too apparent to conceal. In democratic societies, the backlash normally appears in freedom of expression, peaceful demonstrations and in the results of local and general elections.

But what about the helpless, destitute and oppressed people who face hell on earth because of the policies imposed or dictated by remote control? This is the key question that needs to be addressed in the context of violence that appears as a reaction to ongoing injustices in the present-day political arena. Loss of innocent human lives is the most vicious scenario the mind can conceive. Yet, what the mind could not have even conceived for the twenty-first century, the naked eye can now see on television screens day in and day out.

The victims of terror, more often than not, are innocent civilians and, especially, children caught up in hostilities. The so-called civilized world has to carry a burden of guilt for depriving thousands of children of their childhood and for ruthlessly trampling over the rights of innocent children. This situation is rampant in the modern world where the myopic breach of human and civil rights leave bitter memories. Outrage was felt by many people in Iraq against cluster bombs, the use of sophisticated laser-guided missiles and precision bombing with the most imprecise results. The destruction of civilian life is the legacy of modern warfare for the history of the new century.

The killing of innocent people is unequivocally vicious, whether the violence emanates from individual or group or state-sponsored terrorism. Violence emerges as a direct consequence of depriving people of their basic human rights and dispossessing them of the land and wealth which rightfully belongs to them under international law. There are many challenges facing the world community. The solutions to all of them are within the reach of the developed world. What is needed is an unwavering sense of justice and unbiased approach on the part of the nations who have given themselves the right to meddle in the affairs of other countries.

If unfair policies of the powerful nations contribute to the widening gap between rich and poor, this is a recipe for violence. If extravagant wastage of world resources by the monopolists culminates in exploitation of the downtrodden, they are bound to resort to violence. If under the guise of globalization, financial empires are built by robbing poor communities of a decent livelihood, they will be forced into violence. If certain nations are given blind support for depriving indigenous people of the right to live on their own land in peace, then this action is an invitation to the

Chapter 1: Double Standards and Weapons of Mass Distortion

natives to react in violence.

When Israel was given a blank cheque to ignore international law and molest the UN resolutions at will, without the slightest regard for the credibility of the international institutions, then this state of affair was bound to erupt in violence. When American-supplied helicopter gunships showered American missiles at defenceless innocent civilians, many of them children, the bloodbath generated further violence. If 'terrorism' means targeting civilians, without distinguishing combatants from noncombatants, then the results of every single armed conflict in the modern world has to be evaluated in the context of this definition.

On 15 February 2003, peace-loving people in 600 cities around the world protested against war. London witnessed the largest post-World War II demonstration. Many American cities were inundated with protests on a massive scale. From the speeches delivered in the rallies in Britain and the United States, one could witness and feel that the world was not devoid of peace-loving, respectable men of good conscience from different races and faiths. Ken Livingstone the Mayor of London, and Tony Benn the left-wing Labour MP, among other anti-war pioneers, addressed the gathering of two million people. The masses poured into London from all parts of the country expressing their desire and commitment to peace for all the inhabitants of the world.

Ken Livingstone, through his impressive oratory, exposed the double standards of the big nations who enforce the UN resolutions selectively and discriminately. He said, they exempt Israel from any supervision over its nuclear arsenal and weapons of mass destruction although the head of the Israeli government, Ariel Sharon, has committed war crimes in the refugee camps. Tony Benn presented interesting information that a handful of billionaire families are controlling half the wealth of the world.

The US supplies Israel with the latest and most advanced deadly artillery in the world, which Israel has used, not against a regular army, but against stone-throwing youths and civilians. The world has been witnessing malignant collective punishment meted out to the entire people by deliberately depriving them of their livelihood. The Arabs were expected to suffer in silence, patiently and obediently, the heavy-handed policies of Israel.

The American 'road map' is supposed to promote peace in the troubled region. But actions speak louder than words. The 'road map' is not negotiable, yet Sharon recorded more than a dozen objections. From the very day he attended the summit at Aqaba, he escalated his pre-emptive strikes, arbitrary arrests and demolition of houses in the occupied territories. It was possible to carry out a litmus test to find out the sincerity and commitment of Sharon for a permanent settlement to the Middle East crisis. Had the question of the return of the refugees to their forcibly seized lands, and the recognition of the legal status of Jerusalem, been placed right at the top of the agenda, this would immediately have unmasked how serious Sharon was to pursue a peaceful solution.

All along, Sharon declared that the return of the refugees is out of the question, as is withdrawal from Jerusalem. Cessation of settlements in the occupied territories is likewise out of the question. He has been declaring that the three most contentious issues in the peace process are beyond discussion. Does this attitude portray goodwill?

On 1 July 2003, as Sharon was meeting Mahmoud Abbas in Jerusalem for some niceties, the Israeli bulldozers destroyed a mosque in the occupied territories claiming that it had been built illegally. These measures were adopted in compliance with an Israeli court order. But the same courts would never dare to issue orders for the dismantling of settlements in compliance with international law.

The theatrics at Sharm-el-Sheikh and Aqaba were designed to leave charming memories for the Bush campaign in the next presidential race. If comprehensive peace in the region was the motive, then the front-line states, Syria and Lebanon that do have substantial Palestinian refugee populations, would have been invited to participate. However, the US, on the insistence of Israel, decided to keep them isolated, knowing very well that a comprehensive settlement without their direct involvement would not be possible.

The exclusion of Syria and Lebanon can be interpreted in one of two ways. Either the US wants to keep its military option against

Chapter 1: Double Standards and Weapons of Mass Distortion

Syria and Lebanon open, which perfectly suits the Sharonites in Tel Aviv and Washington. Or the US wants to keep the phobia of 'Israel fighting for its life' alive so that the tax-free charity of billions of dollars flowing from the US and Europe does not dry up, which again, perfectly suits the Sharonites.

The 'road map', instead of cementing the loopholes, has appeared to have many snags. On CBC Radio commentary on 28 May 2003, Andrea Anderson said that the Palestinians have called it a 'road map' to nowhere. The Israeli settlers have called it a 'road map' to hell.

The settlements in the West Bank alone have increased by 91 percent since Oslo in 1993. The apartheid wall built by Israel is "twice as high and three times as long as the Berlin Wall".[6] It is naïve to assume that Israel, which has refused to abide by 68 UN resolutions and the US, which has used its veto power only in favour of Israel, would all of a sudden have a change of heart, and that too, one year before the campaign for the presidential election is due to begin.

Had Israel been genuinely interested in peace, then it would have abandoned its half-a-century-old policy of intransigence and obstinacy, which has left scars from the wounds inflicted on the life of the oppressed civilians. It should have demonstrated its goodwill by stopping all the cruelties in the occupied territories. Out of all the people, if the Palestinian and Israeli mothers had felt each other's common pain and anxiety, then the politicians would not have dared to terrorize the life of civilians. Israeli mothers should have been able to feel the agony of Palestinian mothers who were left without a roof over their and their children's heads because of Sharon's craze for demolition.

Due to repressive policies, the life of Palestinian youths has been completely shattered with detrimental consequences for both the communities. No Israeli mother would have wanted to see the aspirations of her young ones crushed under the heavy armoury, F14s and air-to-surface missiles. But this is precisely what has been happening to the Palestinian youths, who in the prime of their life, were robbed of the opportunity to gain education and be employed to

Chapter 1: Double Standards and Weapons of Mass Distortion

fulfil their ambitions in life. The life of children has been devastated with missiles, rockets and helicopter gunship attacks. These memories cannot fade with the passage of time. They generate nothing but resentment.

Despite the fact that the stone-throwing youths were no match compared to the might of the most powerful army in the region, the mental torment of hostilities was emerging on the Israeli side as well. The soldiers of the Israeli army adopted non-conventional methods to express their guilt. The Israeli army now has one of the highest rates of suicide in the world.

At the implementation level of the 'road map', classic delaying tactics have been adopted. On the visit of the Palestinian Prime Minister to Washington in July 2003, the White House spokesman said that the 'security wall' was 'problematic'. This was followed by the Israeli Prime Minister's visit. At the end of his visit, Washington completely tuned down its superficial objection. Hence, Israel was contented that it could continue with its provocative policies of apartheid enclaves and arbitrary arrests despite the ceasefire. The delicacy of the situation was shelved and the lives of children were put at risk once again.

Joe MacAnthony writes: "There are many reasons why Israel has gotten itself into its present pickle ...You cannot sustain a policy that justifies killing children on the West Bank on the one hand while condemning it when the murders occur in Jerusalem." He goes on to write that "officially sponsored assassination" cannot be justified and its repercussion is bound to "haunt every member of the government that stood with it."[7]

President Bush turned a cold shoulder in the first two years of his presidency to any kind of peace processes between the Palestinians and the Israelis. This invigorated the obstinacy of Sharon's extremist government. The region was left ablaze and in the meantime, the US waged war on Afghanistan under the pledge of 'war on terror'. The job was half done, and the US went to war with Iraq in search of weapons of mass destruction. The objective remained totally unaccomplished, and yet, the Pentagon and the State Department started giving signals to Lebanon, Syria and Iran that

Chapter 1: Double Standards and Weapons of Mass Distortion

they were next on the list.

The killing of innocent civilians wherever, and by whoever, and for whatever, and in whichever way, would remain a stigma on the nations calling themselves civilized. No person in his right state of mind can tolerate this reprehensible scenario. Thousands of innocent lives have been unnecessarily lost. Many more thousands face the torments of physical and mental disability. The true effects of the undiagnosed diseases and psychological effects of heavy bombardment on Afghanistan and Iraq are yet to surface. Diseases like the Gulf War Syndrome are yet to be diagnosed.

Before invading Iraq, the Bush officials gave enough hints that they were in the business of changing the map and political landscape of the Middle East. From the rhetoric of the US Defence Secretary, National Security Advisor and Secretary of State, it seems that Iraq is going to be used as a base for launching ambitious crusades on a number of countries on the hit list. The US stampeded over every legal and moral argument against war on Iraq. In its rush to go to war with Iraq, it humiliated Dr Hans Blix, the UN weapons inspector, by implying that his failure to find weapons of mass destruction meant that Saddam had fooled him.[8]

After the war on Iraq, when the noose tightened on the British and the American governments for using faulty intelligence, unreliable reports and doubtful dossiers to justify the war, they responded with further telltale. Public opinion in both countries was bombarded with a barrage of contradictory statements. The public was told that in a country as wide as California, time is needed to find weapons of mass destruction. However, this is precisely what Dr Hans Blix had been saying all along. The Bush Administration was not prepared to give time to the experts for one simple reason. It was neither consciously nor unconsciously prepared to hear that there were no weapons of mass destruction in Iraq.

Donald Rumsfeld, the US Secretary of Defence, came up with a story that the Iraqi dictator might have destroyed his stockpile of weapons of mass destruction just before the war started. The story would have been feasible if Saddam's mind had become unbalanced in his last days in power. If so, why would the US be prepared to pay

$25 million for the head of a lunatic? The purpose for going to war with Iraq was declared loudly, clearly and repeatedly, which was to find and destroy weapons of mass destruction. Now that nothing has been found, the US is trying to use the discovery of mass graves as justification for war. The US already knew about the summary executions in Iraq at least, since 1991. Yet, there is an attempt at politicizing the agony of the deeply aggrieved people.

After the pronouncements of Rumsfeld, President Bush came up with a story that Saddam might have allowed weapons of mass destruction to be stolen. This was a credible story provided these weapons could be stored in wardrobes or bank vaults. The public has already been told that no smoking gun has to exist for weapons of mass destruction to exist. True. They need not even have to be smuggled out of Iraq. After all, the anthrax scare was initiated by US army personnel, and was, therefore, suppressed and forgotten. If an Arab or Muslim were implicated for possessing anthrax, he would have ended up in Guantanamo Bay.

Under the agenda of the neoconservatives, Iraq will be used as a springboard to target other countries in the area. If 'democracy' still incorporates the clause 'for the people, of the people and by the people', then the US military occupation of Iraq has not shown any prospects for democracy in that country as yet. The unholy alliance of the Israeli-infatuated new breed of neoconservatives, eminently placed in the Bush Administration, is instrumental in pursuing aggressive and hawkish policies. In the process, the classical admonition of the founding father of the Union has been undermined.

Abraham Lincoln, the sixteenth President of the United States said in his Second Inaugural Address on 4 March 1865: "With malice toward none; with charity for all; with firmness in the right, let us strive on to finish the work we are in; …to care for him who shall have borne the battle, and for his widow, and his orphan – to do all which may achieve and cherish a just, and a lasting peace, among ourselves, and with all nations." This may sound Chinese to those who are intoxicated with the crusading offensive against sovereign nations.

Chapter 1: Double Standards and Weapons of Mass Distortion

The rationale presented to the public is that the United States went into war in Afghanistan and Iraq and is threatening Iran, for the sake of liberation, democracy, weapons of mass destruction, human rights and combating terrorism. No mention is being made that the barons who committed the US in its ongoing wars, have deep vested interest in the arms industry, the world of finance, the oil and construction industries. Both Bush Junior and Senior represent the oil industry of Texas. It is a strange coincidence that Jay Garner, the first US-appointed military ruler of Iraq, is an arms consultant and a great friend of Israel, which is engaged in an age-old political conflict with Arab countries. Is the public being told the truth?

An anomalous circumstance arises where a lie is hammered constantly and intensively into the minds of the people, so that they start to believe that it is the truth. The Arabs and Muslims are victims of such an anomaly in as much as the American people are. An intentional lie of the Iraqi connection with September 11 was so effective that according to the polls, two-thirds of Americans believed that Saddam carried out the atrocity of September 11. The same proportion also believed that Iraqi hijackers were on board the hijacked planes.[9]

A lie that is injected with tact and cunningness could spread like wildfire. It may take many years to reach the attention of all those people who may have been misled. Even then, the impression left by false information on the psyche of the people may not be obliterated altogether. Some people would be prone to reject the truth and remain adamant in believing the lies.

2

Iraq Between Two Human Rights Disasters

THE tale of Iraq is a tale of two calamities. One calamity is called Saddam who was first nurtured and then dumped by the United States after he outlived his usefulness. He squandered the enormous wealth of Iraq to build a personal empire for himself, his sons and his tribesmen. He was ferocious in annihilating anything and everything that acted as an obstacle between him and his burning ambition.

In June 2003, *Al-Arabiya* televised several documentaries and analyses of the personal profile of Saddam, giving an insight into the self-love, self-glory, self-gratification and extravagance on which he built his image to the absolute detriment of the Iraqi nation. This Machiavellian rogue betrayed Iraq by robbing the riches and wealth of the nation for his and his family's personal benefit whilst his countrymen starved and died in millions.

The personal profile of his sons in *Al-Arabiya* reflected how successful Saddam was in bringing them up in his own image. A maidservant and a special bodyguard of Uday, who were interviewed on the programme, gave an inside story of his evil psychology. They said, he killed people with his own hands. Being the son of a mass-murderer, this was perhaps his privilege, in addition to controlling the drugs trade, and smuggling the wealth of Iraq outside the country. In the all-night dancing and drinking parties hosted by Saddam's sons, the abducted women were forced to dance for their pleasure. If there was any feeling at all for the humanitarian tragedy that had befallen the children of Iraq during the decade of embargo, no responsible government official could have even remotely engaged in lavish parties that were hosted by Saddam's sons. Those who attended their funeral are best placed to answer, how much of their extravagant luxuries and looted property have they been able to take with them to their graves?

Chapter 2: Iraq between Two Human Rights Disasters

Another calamity for Iraq is the sinister design of war that was planned long before September 11. The betrothal between radical Zionists and Christian extremists under the umbrella of 'neoconservatives' gained prominence in the Bush Administration. They succeeded in pushing their expansionist ambition forward. Among many hard-core supporters of Israel, Michael Ledeen, a prominent neoconservative activist, who has close connections with the White House, promotes through his numerous articles, weird ideas about American supremacy and America's evolutionary right to invade any country. His articles are posted on the website of the American Enterprise Institute for Public Policy Research (AEI). The relationship of this think-tank and the Pentagon was explored in the BBC *Panorama* programme.[10]

Speaking from the platform of the Jewish Institute for National Security Affairs (JINSA) on 30 April 2003, Ledeen, who is referred as 'the Guru of Neoconservatives', preached aggression against sovereign members of the United Nations – Iran, Syria and Lebanon. Dick Cheney, Donald Rumsfeld and Paul Wolfowitz quote his ideas.[11] Ledeen was taught by his professor at the University of Wisconsin that the "Western countries had been suffocated and could only be revived through Fascism and Nazism".[12]

The US Secretary of Defence, Donald Rumsfeld, appointed his deputy, Paul Wolfowitz, to head the new intelligence agency called Office of Special Plans (OSP). Its function was to devise a strategy for the new century to "fight and decisively win multiple, simultaneous major theatre wars."[13] It is said that Wolfowitz was the main architect of the war against Iraq. The unilateralism of the US has been a subject of international outcry since September 11. *The Guardian* wrote that in the view of Richard Perle and Paul Wolfowitz, "...all that counts is the overwhelming power of the US." It further states that the UN is facing a crisis because of the US power of veto. The US has destabilized the Middle East, "wrecked Nato" and "sabotaged the EU".[14]

The headlines in *USA Today* on Wolfowitz's testimony to the Senate Committee read, "US troops may be in Iraq for 10 years: defense officials reportedly seek up to $54 billion a year".[15]

Chapter 2: Iraq between Two Human Rights Disasters

However, on 7 September 2003, President Bush asked the Congress to approve $87 billion for Iraq, raising the US budget deficit to over $500 billion. Nobody has ever suggested that this amount would be treated as a charity. If Iraq did not have the second largest reserve of oil in the world, would the US have invaded the country in the first place? The Liberians have been desperately appealing that they consider the US soldiers as their 'father' and respect them as such, yet the US was very reluctant to send in its troops. Would the US have hesitated if Liberia was an oil-producing country? These are the questions that the public has a democratic right to ask and the policy-makers have a democratic obligation to answer.

The total cost of invading Iraq is expected to rise to almost $700 billion. With the annual US Budget deficit running at over $500 billion and set to rise substantially in the next five years, any economist worth his salt is bound to ask, how is the United States going to repay its debts? The cost of maintaining the US troops in Iraq is $4.6 billion a month. The cynics might suggest that the invasion of Afghanistan and Iraq and the destabilizing plan against Iran, Syria and Lebanon, not to mention Saudi Arabia, could all be part of the long-term strategy.

After occupying Iraq, the coalition forces resented being called the 'occupying force'. They preferred to be called 'liberators', not even 'conquerors'. Then they changed their mind. Under the Geneva Convention and international charters, they could not have possibly taken upon themselves the responsibility of rebuilding Iraq and milking the enormous benefits associated therewith, unless they accepted the status of 'occupiers'.

The legal status of the occupiers was to make sure that apart from the Oil Ministry, other key organs of the state also got full protection. Nevertheless, within the reach of the American forces, Iraq was stripped of its rich history and rare treasures. The Museum, the Central Library and the University in Baghdad were being looted in broad daylight. The American forces did not even lift a finger to stop the daytime robbery. Despite constant pleas from various non-governmental organizations abroad, the Americans were not interested in moving their tanks a mere fifty yards to protect the

Museum and the Central Library. Rumsfeld shocked the observers in the field as well as the international reporters and TV viewers, by bashing at the world media for exaggerating the tales of destruction and looting. He called it a "celebration of freedom" by the Iraqis.

The rebuilding of Iraq by the occupation forces is bound to create jobs and open up employment opportunities for the skilled workers of the occupying powers. Their manufacturers can look forward to gaining lucrative contracts. Their experts can look forward to charging rocketing fees for consultancy. Nobody has to worry that they will be hounded by protracted auditing regulations. So long as Iraq has the means of paying hundreds of billions of dollars for its reconstruction, there was nothing to worry about. A bizarre procedure was followed for awarding the rebuilding contracts, without any bidding or international tender. The bulk of these contracts, where the US was poised to benefit economically, were awarded even before the war started. In contrast, the US was completely unprepared and did not have any plan of action on how to deal with the post-war collapse of civil and emergency services that were to cause chaos in Iraq.

Robert Fisk writes with his impressive journalistic flair: "...[M]anagement of port of Umm Qasr has been grabbed...by a US company, one of whose lobbyists just happens to have been President George Bush's deputy assistant when he was governor of Texas. ...Dick Cheney's old company, has major contracts to extinguish oil fires in Iraq. ...The most likely giant to hoover up the reconstruction contract is Bechtel whose senior vice president ...serves on President Bush's defence policy board. This is the same Bechtel which...once helped Saddam build a plant for manufacturing ethylene. ...On the Board of Bechtel sits former secretary of state George Schultz, who again just happens to be chairman of the advisory board of the Committee for the Liberation of Iraq..."[16]

The *Toronto Star* wrote that the cost of restoration of the oil production contract, awarded to Vice President Dick Cheney's past company Halliburton, was raised from $76.7 million to $184.7 million within a month. The report says: "Several members of the U.S. Congress have invoked Cheney's name to raise the hint of favouritism..." The company has also received a military work contract of over $600 million. Halliburton's subsidiary K.B.R has been awarded over $500 million worth of contract for what it calls "troop support service".[17]

Reuters reported that the US and UK-based oil giants took a large chunk of the tender for the sale of oil after the war. Royal Dutch/Shell was awarded two million barrels of Basra Light Crude. The tender closed on 7 July 2003. Chevron Texaco will ship six million barrels to the US West Coast. However, the US faces a number of cumbersome legal dilemmas in reviving Iraq's oil industry to its full potential, which is expected to cost $30 - $40 billion. The reluctance of oil giants to inject huge capital is explained by Sir Phillip Watts, chairman of Royal Dutch/Shell. In order to enter contracts which will be prolonged for many years, security and legitimate negotiating authority has to be in place.[18] At present, the lawlessness and chaos allows the Iraqi oil to be smuggled in tankers through the gulf. Neither now nor during the tyranny of Saddam did the people of Iraq benefited from the most important natural resource the country has.

Iraq's financial system and retail banking are also the likely areas for overhaul. J. P. Morgan Chase & Co., Citigroup and Bank of America are already lining up to participate in the process. With the country's gross national product valued at about $29 billion prior to war, and oil revenues expected to fetch around $18 billion a year,[19] this was another fertile field waiting for exploration. Initially the American and British governments stressed that the oil revenues would be kept in trust for the Iraqi people in escrow account under UN supervision. Then they sought UN approval to supervise the account themselves.

The consequence of refusing a UN-sponsored administration in Iraq by the coalition made the occupation forces susceptible to a number of civil and criminal law suits. David Scheffer writes in the *Financial Times:* "Occupation law was never intended to encourage invasion and occupation for the purpose of transforming a society...". He identifies the failure of the US and UK forces to provide humanitarian and civil amenities despite the fact that "an invasion and its many responsibilities were readily foreseeable – as is the case in Iraq, whose invasion was planned for a long time."[20]

Iraq faces an onslaught of footing the bill for every rocket and every laser-guided missile fired at the Iraqi cities during the war. With oil revenues falling under the direct management of the Americans, Iraq may assist in rescuing the US economy, which could be rescued by neither the fiscal policy, nor the monetary or economic policy, since President Bush assumed power in a spectacular election circus.

Economic and political factors played a vital role in taking the decision to go to war. In the United States, interest and tax revenues are at the hub of controlling and gearing the economy towards government defined objectives. Thirteen reductions brought the interest rate at 1%, to its lowest level in half a century. Yet, the economy has not been revived. Large chunks of tax revenues were refunded to the American taxpayers, but painfully failed to revive the economy from its worst post-World War recession.

The think-tank pondered over the innovations to rescue the US economy before the next presidential election. Otherwise, there was a real risk that Bush Junior might have to face the same destiny as Bush Senior. The imperialist cards were already on the table. The neoconservatives grasped this unrivalled opportunity to translate their war plans into action.

The hawkish thinking started to unfold. If the United Nations was hesitant to submit to the will of Washington, then it was not performing its duty. If the international community was not prepared to approve a second resolution endorsing war on Iraq, then the world was failing to fight terrorism. The US was embarking on a 'democratization' adventure, in which, France and Germany among others, were expected to be submissive.

The Arab world was expected to take lessons in democratic values from the sources acceptable to Washington or else be prepared for grim consequences. If the Arabs preferred to have localized training, then the only democracy that the Middle East has begotten was just round the corner. They could demonstrate their goodwill at least by sharing espionage activities on the Islamic

Chapter 2: Iraq between Two Human Rights Disasters

parties.

The coalition set out to twist the arm of the outlaw in Baghdad, who had been an outlaw from the very day that the US imposed him on the Iraqi people. The dictator provided the coalition with every excuse they were looking for to wage war on Iraq. No approval of the Security Council was needed. No justification under international law was sought. No concurrence of the close allies was necessary. There was a mission to be fulfilled and that was to remove any assumed threat to the security of Israel. Top US politicians stated this openly during and after the war. In the real world, Saddam was never a threat to the security of the US or Israel. Those who were not able to present any evidence except hearsay concocted his connection to Al-Qaeda. The outcome of the war, as expected, proved that empty drums that make a lot of noise eventually fail to deliver. The Socialist Ba'ath party had spread its venom to every layer of Iraqi society for over three decades and at the end, it landed in the ditch of anathema.

There would not have been any need to uproot the despot of Iraq at the cost of thousands of innocent civilian lives, had he not been installed in the first place. Paradoxically, those who supplied him with weapons of mass destruction, still have the audacity to face the public. He and his political party needed chemical and biological weapons only for use against the Iraqi people. Such was the game they played throughout their demonic reign in order to stay in power.

In its midnight news on the eve of the New Year (2003), *Sky News* TV showed archive pictures of the meeting that took place between Saddam and Rumsfeld in the early 1980s. The report accompanying the film-clip was all the more interesting as it was based on declassified information. The US had agreed to supply Saddam with chemical and biological weapons for the purpose of stopping the advance of the Iranian troops in the Iran - Iraq war. The memorable photograph of Rumsfeld shaking hands with Saddam, declassified by the National Security Archives, was selected by the California Peace Action in its advertising campaign in Washington's Metro transit system.[21]

Jeremy Scahill in his interesting article in *CommonDreams*

writes that in December 1983, for the first time since the 1967 Arab - Israeli war, Rumsfeld was the key figure to have patched up relations between Washington and Saddam. He was deputed by President Ronald Reagan for this mission. The US told the Gulf States that the defeat of Iraq in its war against Iran was against the US interest and it would ensure that this did not occur. As Rumsfeld was visiting Iraq the UPI reported from the United Nations that, "Mustard gas…has been used on Iranian soldiers…" Commenting on Rumsfeld's desire to run for the '1988 Republican Presidential nomination', *Chicago Tribune* listed among his achievements, the restoration of relations between the US and Iraq, notwithstanding the fact that Saddam was notorious for using chemical weapons and nerve gases against the Iranians troops. At a time when Saddam was terrorizing his own people in 1982, the US removed Iraq from the list of nations sponsoring terrorism, and hence, opened up a world of opportunity for the US corporations competing to sell helicopters and heavy arms. When Saddam attacked the Kurds with chemical bombs from the US-supplied helicopters, the White House blocked the Senate proposal for imposing sanctions. Scahill further writes that according to extensive research carried out, Rumsfeld did not issue even a remote condemnation for Saddam's use of chemical bombs.[22]

When chemical bombs rained on Halabjah on the Kurdish population, there was an attempt to suppress the news. The matter was raised in the British Parliament, but the government of the time pretended that it did not know anything.

The University of Sussex student magazine *The Badger,* obtained the US Senate documents which establish a connection between Washington and Saddam's regime. Geoffrey Holland writes that he undertook upon himself a tireless effort of communicating with the members of Parliament on this issue. The article makes similar disclosures as the *Sky News* had done on New Year's Eve. Rumsfeld as a member of the President's General Advisory Committee on Arms Control in the 1980s, agreed to supply anthrax to Saddam. He has of course denied supplying biological weapons to the disgraced Iraqi dictator. However, the Senate's Riegle Report from Washington proves that the US supplied "seven batches of anthrax to Iraq between 8 February 1985 and 29 September 1988", writes Mr Holland. His article, posted on the homepage of Paul Flynn, MP, pinpoints the responsibility for the official cover-up of such vital information.[23]

During and after the war on Iraq, many cities suffered from an acute shortage of clean drinking water and medicines with a potential health hazard. Power cuts have continued even during the scorching summer heat. After the war, the residents of Baghdad did not have flour to make bread for their children. There was an acute shortage of medicines in hospitals. Nevertheless the priority of the occupiers was not restoration of basic amenities. The coalition, by failing to address the bare minimum daily needs of the ordinary people, made more enemies than friends.

The reputable American *Time* magazine made alarming disclosures on the intentional damage caused to the Iraqi property by the American troops. The vast scale of looting and vandalism at Baghdad Airport was perpetuated and the soldiers themselves were instrumental in looting the goods from the duty-free shops. Five Boeing aircrafts stationed at the airport were rendered nonfunctional. They ripped out the planes' fixture and fittings, cockpit machinery and equipment. The US estimates that the damage might be worth as much as $100 million.[24] If the malicious damage is repaired at all, it would be Iraq that would have to pay the cost with interest.

Eight weeks after the end of the war, the Parliament in Britain and the Congress in the US started questioning whether their governments had misled the public by using unreliable intelligence. The reason given to the lawmakers for going to war, simply did not match the aftermath realities on the ground. There was disquiet in the media. Did the governments lie and deceive the public? Was the decision to go to war based on scrambled evidence in the first place? Paul Krugman writes in the *New York Times*: "A similar process of ...choosing and exaggerating intelligence that suited the administration's preconceptions, unfolded over the issues of W.M.D's before the war." The hawks had already made up their mind and it did not matter that Blair's dossier was flawed or Powell's presentation at the United Nations was unconvincing. There was

Chapter 2: Iraq between Two Human Rights Disasters

nervousness in the intelligence community as "...former U.S. intelligence officials began warning that official pronouncements were being based on 'cooked intelligence' "[25]

Democrat Senator, Carl Levin of Michigan on the Senate Armed Services Committee accused the CIA of, as he put it, "deliberately misleading United Nations inspectors to help clear the decks for an invasion of Iraq."[26]

Information contained in President Bush's State of the Union address in January 2003 on Saddam having obtained tons of 'yellowcake uranium' from Niger, was based on forged documents. Condoleezza Rice, the National Security Advisor, confessed that the intelligence information on which the President relied was "not credible".[27] Analysts in the intelligence agencies were annoyed that senior personnel in the Administration picked and chose to disclose, what they called, "classified intelligence reports that supported the worst-case scenario concerning Iraq's weapons programs, making it seem as if there was an imminent threat to the United States".[28]

Officials have declared that the US is planning to keep four bases in Iraq: one near Baghdad airport, another near Nasiriyah in the South, the third in the remote western desert and the fourth in the Kurdish area in the North.[29] If this was a long-term goal, it had to be connected with an issue which would sell well to the American people. Hence, it was claimed that Iraq posed a threat to the security of the United States.

A similar attempt was made to sell the scare on Iran to the American public, that the country is developing a nuclear bomb and harbouring terrorists. Charley Reese writes: "But if it was dead wrong about Iraq, why should we believe anything it says about Iran."[30] Yet, unilateral threats of military action on Iran's nuclear facilities have escalated even though the Bush Administration failed to convince the Board of the International Atomic Energy Agency to condemn Iran outright. But the directorate of the IAEA succumbed to the political pressures from Washington and harmonized its voice with that reverberating from the State Department. In contrast, post-retirement pronouncements of Dr Hans Blix indicate that here was a man who stood firm and courageous in his professional duties in the face of ridicule and political pressure. The chairman of the IAEA finally broke his silence on 27 August 2003 and accused Washington of double-standards for non-containment of nuclear proliferation.

If there is any lesson to be drawn from the experience of Iraq, then it must be recognized that the world as a whole has to be free from weapons of mass destruction. No matter in whose hands they are, they are unsafe, simply because the political oscillations of the powerful nations cannot be trusted. The moral standards of these nations swing like a pendulum to suit their own interest. Albert Einstein has rightly said: "I know not with what weapons World War III will be fought, but World War IV will be fought with sticks and stones."

Having entrenched itself on Iraqi soil, the US has assumed a supreme right to determine the future of Iraq. *The Independent* of 10 May 2003 gave coverage to Bush and Blair's broken promises on control of Iraq's oil, on weapons inspection, on humanitarian aid and on their role as the occupying power.

Washington changed its mind on running the country. Superficially, Russia and France emerged as the good guys of the Security Council when they spoke eloquently against the war. But as Washington appointed itself the *de facto* ruler of Iraq, the tone of their voice started to crack. They were already worried about losing billions of dollars worth of contracts they had signed with Saddam. Perhaps next time round they should learn to shop around for representative governments to rely on.

Even the Germans who were against the war, agreed with the US about lifting the sanctions. The Russians were concerned more than anything else about their massive debts. At a time when Russia was in economic tatters, with crippled currency and huge loans looming over its head from Western financial institutions, why did it care to lend billions to Saddam's government? This explains why the Russians remained reserved throughout the crisis.

The US was desperately in need to lift the sanctions. It required the support of the Russians and the French and other Security Council members to get the resolution through in the United Nations. After several amendments, accepted by the US, the resolution was finally passed on 22 May 2003. Hence, the right of Russia, France and Germany to share in the spoils of war was recognized but not formulized. Russia itself divulged its secret that it sold its vote in the Security Council about the lifting of sanctions in exchange for recognition of its debts by the occupation forces. In this way, the US got what it wanted and Russia got what it wanted. The booty would be shared from Iraq's resources.

As part of the process of sharing the booty, Jose Maria Aznar, the Prime Minister of Spain was not to be left out. He decided to send his Spanish brigade of 2000 soldiers to patrol the city of Najaf in Iraq. But he was to pass an additional message. His brigade was to bear the Cross of St James of Compostela, known as 'the Moor Killer', who had guided the medieval Christians to conquer Spain from the Muslims.[31] The people of Iraq had already suffered humiliation from Saddam's forces, and now it was the turn of the coalition to spread salt on their wounds.

An anonymous commander of the disgraced republican guards, in his interview on *Al-Jazeerah* on 10 May 2003, alleged betrayal and treason on the part of the Iraqi authorities. The culprits remained at large as mass graves of Iraqi citizens, who were summarily executed with shots in their heads, were being found. Shocking tales of tormented men and women were being told in several TV documentaries. If any credibility is to be given to the international judicial system, the effort has to be multiplied to find the perpetrators of these crimes against humanity. They have to be brought to justice.

The hawks in Washington have struggled hard to establish a connection between Osama Bin Laden and Saddam, notwithstanding the fact that Bin Laden considered Saddam a heretic and infidel.

A new episode has commenced in the sufferings of the Iraqi people. They had to endure collective punishment imposed on them by the world community for over twelve years. When it was time to take charge of their affairs, Rumsfeld explicitly spelled out that an Islamic government will not be acceptable to the US. This is equivalent to saying that the US would not tolerate a system or culture based on Judaism in Israel, something that Rumsfeld even

Chapter 2: Iraq between Two Human Rights Disasters

under his dreadful nightmare would not dare to declare. Under which UN resolution or Geneva Convention or humanitarian law has Rumsfeld bestowed upon himself the authority to dictate what system the Iraqis must or must not choose?

How long it will take for the tragic plight of the Iraqi people to improve despite the lifting of sanctions, needs to be seen. What the UN sanctions did to the poor children of Iraq during that period will go down in history as one of the cruelest treatments ever meted out to children. In the words of Madeleine Albright, the US Secretary of State in the Clinton Administration in 1996, it was a price worth paying. These sanctions killed over one million civilians, including half-a-million children under the age of five.[32]

Saddam, his family and friends were least affected by the sanctions. If they had any sense of patriotism, they would have abdicated. With no human values to worry about, they were determined to cling on to power whatever the cost. They sought to deceive international public opinion as they had been deceiving their own people. When the noose tightened round them, they resorted to cheap tactics to prove their legitimacy. In a hurriedly orchestrated election, with Saddam as the only candidate for presidency, none other than his once-upon-a-time Vice-President, Izzat Ibrahim Al-Douri, with grey hair but no sense of shame, came up with farcical election results. All the eleven million odd eligible voters had unanimously voted for Saddam. All the insane in the country turned sane for that day. There was no absenteeism. No person had fallen ill on the Election Day, no one had dropped dead and no voter was occupying a hospital bed. Every single registered voter was physically present. However, the drama failed to play the trick even with the long experience of Izzat Ibrahim in the service of the tyrant.

The Iraqi people were quite capable of getting rid of these foreign-sponsored elements from power. They had risen in 1991, without any outside involvement, to flush out the dictator who was leading the nation from one disastrous war to another. But as a result of the betrayal of George Bush Senior, 300,000 people were slaughtered in cold-blood. In the wake of what was claimed to be the Iranian threat, the US decided to leave Saddam in power, so that the nervous oil-producing countries in the region could willingly offer a foothold to the US. This policy proved to be suicidal for both.

In the week-long programme on *Al-Arabiya* TV network in early May, Mohammad al-Douri, the ex-representative of Iraq in the United Nations was the guest of honour. A lady was so overcome by his performance at the UN that she phoned him on the programme and offered him the job of becoming the next President of Iraq. In answer to a question from a viewer, he enumerated some of the positive and constructive contributions of the dictator. Among these were that he built bridges, roads, schools, hospitals and so forth. What type of impression was being created on the viewers that Saddam was a philanthropic person? Did he spend millions from his personal wealth? Was he doing a favour to the Iraqi people? Was he providing a charitable service? Was he doing something more than what he was expected to do with the enormous wealth of the nation? For every bridge he built, he built a palace for himself and his sons. For every hospital he built, he built prisons, so that his bloodthirsty sons, brothers and cousins could rejoice at the agony and torture of other human beings. Installing Saddam in itself was a crime against humanity.

Such tyrants are imposed by foreign powers through the barrel of a tank and are meant to serve the interest of their masters by sucking the blood out of the veins of their nations. With their arrogance and intoxication for power, they do not care to study the history of human existence on the planet and to derive any moral lesson. It is the duty of the scholars and men of religion to advise their leaders that no unjust and oppressive rulers in the annals of mankind, with all the power and might they could muster, have managed to emerge victorious. Whether he is Nimrod or Pharaoh, Mussolini or Hitler, they were destined to end their lives in disgrace and humiliation.

Saddam and his hedonist gang should have known that human history does not shed any tears for the doom of the dictators. At a time when Iraq was facing the most serious political, economic and humanitarian crisis in its history, the ignominious Saddam kept on building gigantic palaces for himself and his family. Now these

Chapter 2: Iraq between Two Human Rights Disasters

palaces have become headquarters for the American troops.

Saddam shared many characteristic traits with Nero. Whether or not they will share each other's end, only time will tell. Nero once enjoyed the agony of the people of Rome when Rome was burning. He took delight in the trauma that he inflicted on others. Saddam brought disrespect to the superb values and traditions of the Arab people. He was a stigma to the moral teachings of the religion he apparently professed. His crimes against humanity targeted the very people who gave him and his sons the stupendous identity to which they were not entitled. Saddam and his Ba'athist brutes, the collaborators in his vicious crimes, have committed treachery against the people of Iraq. The villains of history cannot and will not be remembered with kind words. The verdict of history is bound to place them in the Chamber of Horrors where they belong.

Almost all the concentration camps of the tyrant have now been opened. The old and infirm parents, counting the last days of their lives, have not given up the slightest hope of meeting their loved ones. They believe that there are underground prison trenches from where their loved ones are crying for rescue. It seems certain that the missing prisoners had been executed without trial and without the knowledge of their next of kin. The lives of noble learned scholars were brutally terminated when they stood bravely against the subjugation of their own countrymen. They refused to lead a cowardly life that preferred to hide at home as humanity screamed for help. In Hindu mythology, a continuous process of demotion is in orbit between the human species and devils. Saddam and his Mafia perfectly fitted with the Hindu myth of demotions.

The grassroots do expect men of knowledge and media to perform their bare minimum humanitarian duty by adopting a stance against the evil behaviour of the rulers, and to stand resolute in demanding respect for the civil rights of the citizens. With the discovery of mass graves, the beastly nature of Saddam's reign is being unveiled.

3

The Sedition of Glorifying the Tyrants and Oppressors

MANY ancient civilizations have been wiped out of existence because of rampant injustices and misuse of power. They indulged in the enslavement and subjugation of other human beings. Only in the recent past, the Soviet empire failed to leave for itself a place even in the dustbin of history, simply because it repeated all the crimes that had doomed other empires. The Socialist and Communist cultures nurtured exploitative economic philosophies. When the hypocrisy of the system was unmasked after the dismantling of the Soviet Union, it was discovered that the leaders had never lived the lifestyle they had been preaching about to their comrades. The people who had supposedly fought the bourgeoisie, turned out to be the concealed bourgeois class themselves, with illegal foreign bank accounts and smuggled wealth, amassed out of the misery of their own people. There is a lesson to be learnt by the Arab and Muslim world from these facts of history.

History provides dazzling evidence that every evil empire and dynastic rule that resorts to arrogance and oppression causes its own downfall. After succeeding for a few years or a few centuries, it eventually meets its fate. In its heyday in order to survive, it endeavours to attract on its side those who are known as the 'right-thinking members of the society', who have the confidence of the grassroots. Among various categories of scholars and men of religion, there are those who, at worst, extend their co-operation to the oppressors, and at best, maintain silence in the face of injustices perpetuated by the rulers who are notorious for abusing their power. The noble souls, who are prepared to proclaim the truth in all circumstances without fearing for their lives, are scarce.

Suppression of the civil rights of the populace becomes possible when scholars and men of religion display their moral weakness and duplicity. The opportunists among them are even

Chapter 3: The Sedition of Glorifying the Tyrants and Oppressors

prepared to auction their soul and self-respect for material gains. Their passive attitude bolsters the resolve of the autocratic rulers to continue their hold on power. For centuries, scholars and men of religion falling under this category have conspired with the rulers in forming a 'mob' mentality. Consequently, people have been customized to accept that in the course of enforceability of law and order, two different standards would apply, one for the public and another for the ruling elites.

If an ordinary member of the public commits theft, adultery or murder, he cannot escape punishment, simply because his hand or head is 'chop able'. If the same offences are committed by the elitists or influential personalities, then the law is allowed to be chopped instead. Small thieves and criminals are subjected to rigid implementation of the law. While big thieves remain unreachable. They secretly earn hefty commissions of millions of dollars on their nation's arms and construction contracts and get the money transferred directly to their Swiss or New York accounts. The masses have been trained to accept such a hypocritical mockery of justice as a norm.

The court-clergy and scholars remain under an illusion that by siding with unjust and despotic rulers, they can succeed in keeping themselves and their family members safe and secure and free from any harm. But when the day of reckoning comes, the deluge engulfs everybody, those who did evil and those who tolerated evil willingly. The vile heritage that Saddam and his gangsters have left behind provides food for thought for the people of understanding in the Arab and Muslim world.

For a long time, the court-clerics have taken undue advantage of their position, and become co-conspirators in prioritizing the iron-fisted reigns of the tyrants over the rights of the people. But the harangue of the court-clerics backfires sooner or later. As people face new realities, they tend to compare their own plight vis-à-vis other communities.

The Arab governments on their part have played a dubious role. Had the Arab nations fulfilled their bare minimum duty and responsibility of containing the bestial reign of the Socialist Ba'ath

Chapter 3: The Sedition of Glorifying the Tyrants and Oppressors

party in Iraq, much of the ensuing devastation would have been averted. Under the very nose of the Arab League, the Ba'athists turned the country and its enormous wealth into a tribal and family enterprise with plans to leave the 'republic' in hereditary succession. Despite commanding one of the most powerful armies in the region, the tyrant totally failed to defend Baghdad even for a day. If Baghdad could fall in such a spectacular way, any Arab capital is susceptible.

The human rights of the aggrieved people are breached when persons who are in a position of trust, prefer to button their lips and assume a conspiracy of silence. With the best of eloquence and oratory in the Friday sermons that are televised on the Arab government TV channels, the core issues are never touched. The court-clerics or the clergy occupying the pulpits, avoid advising their political leaders not to usurp the human rights of citizens, to respect civil liberties and to allow freedom of speech. On the contrary, one would hear them frequently advising the congregation, that whatever their (unelected, unrepresentative and self-imposed) leaders do is in their best interest, and that they are obliged to obey them.

This attitude implies that nobody should dare to ask how much of the country's wealth is wasted on the luxuries of the ruling family. Nobody should dare to demand dispensation of justice on equal grounds between the rulers and the ruled. Nobody should attempt to criticize the rulers for non-transparency of government policies. In this situation, the involvement of the public in the democratic process of running their own country remains out of the question. National wealth belongs to the people and there should, therefore, be full accountability for any mismanagement and misappropriation up to the highest echelon of the ruling and governmental hierarchy. In the Islamic political system, the rulers are the servants and not the masters of the people. This fact is conveniently forgotten.

The 'rubber-stamp' clerics, who justify the follies of their political leaders, are responsible for misleading the masses and keeping them backward. At times the pulpit turns into a platform for airing fizzy propaganda for the ruling class. One quite often hears

Chapter 3: The Sedition of Glorifying the Tyrants and Oppressors

from the pulpits in Friday sermons that anybody who does not obey the 'authority' is a transgressor, a sinner, is outside the fold of the community of believers and dies the death of ignorance. For centuries, such misguidance has forced us, the Muslims, into surrendering our fundamental rights at the hands of the 'authority' who abuses its power. It is only the latter type of 'authority' which is the subject of critical analogy in this study.

To preach obedience to the 'authority' installed in power is not enough. What about the 'authority' that does not live up to the aspirations of the people, tramples on their human rights, curbs their civil liberties, impedes their progress, robs them of the rights to elect their own representatives and breaches every religious and legal covenants? The court-clerics would never suggest even by a slip of the tongue that it is this type of 'authority' that is indulging in sin, is transgressing the Law, is unworthy of obedience, is outside the fold of the community of believers and dies the death of ignorance. Here is a classic example of the criminalization of victims that takes place, not only in the domain of the deceitful political world, but in the purely religious environment.

Up until the unopposed surrender of Baghdad to the American troops, Friday sermons televised from Imam Abu Hanifah mosque, and at times, from Sheikh Abdul Qader Jilani mosque, and from Umm-al-Ma'arek (Mother of the Battles) mosque in Baghdad, on the Iraqi TV, presented the best of exhortations one could hear, soothing on the ear and refreshing for the heart. At the end, the imams of the mosques would pour acid on whatever they had said, by praising and praying vehemently for the fascist dictator. Had there been anything pleasing to God in their invocation for their 'great brave mujahid' and their 'great victor', as they used to refer to Saddam, then their prayers would not have been thrown back in their faces. They thought that they would succeed in fooling God as they have been fooling simple-minded people in the congregation. One imam of the mosque even used to brandish from the pulpit an open sword in the name of his 'great leader'. The leader eventually proved his 'greatness' by absconding from the battlefield. The sword, too, disappeared with him. It is very easy to make garbled noises in the

Chapter 3: The Sedition of Glorifying the Tyrants and Oppressors

name of 'jihad' so long as others are pushed forward to sacrifice themselves and the provocateurs remain safe and sound in hiding. When oppressors are characterized as the exemplary models from the pulpits, then such clerics take the blame for whatever calamity befalls the nation and its people.

Some people might claim that these imams of the mosques after all, were under compulsion and threat from the *mukhabarat* (secret police) to praise Saddam or else face grave consequences. But this is not the whole truth. This claim can be dismissed from what transpired on Friday, 18 July 2003 in Baghdad. The imam of Umm-al-Ma'arek mosque demanded in his sermon a general amnesty for the Ba'athist leaders and condemned the declaration of the day Saddam fell from power as National Day. The complicity is self-explanatory.

In the aftermath of the killing of Saddam's two sons, Uday and Qusay, a cleric mentioned in his Friday sermon from Beirut that they died as 'martyrs'. After the fall of Baghdad, the Arabic and non-Arabic media and press have shed enormous light on the bestial criminal nature of Saddam and his two sons. Therefore, this cleric and others of his type cannot possibly pretend to be unaware, unless they prefer to remain ignorant. If the occupants of the pulpits cannot even feel a minimal sense of justice for the ladies who were abducted and raped by the gangsters of Uday, then the pulpits have to be relieved of these accessories to crimes. Such clerics would never have branded the two brothers as martyrs had ladies from their own household been abducted. As long as others were wronged and treated savagely, it did not matter to them. Pulpits are overburdened with those who are prepared to justify every crime committed by the ruling clique on condition that they and their family-members are not among the victims.

The tales of how God will forgive mass-murderers have started appearing on fairly responsible Muslim websites in the aftermath of the killing of Uday and Qusay. As their long and bloody careers were in progress, these very organizations had hypocritically assumed indifference to the humanitarian afflictions that had affected thousands. Imagine what the irresponsible Muslim websites have

Chapter 3: The Sedition of Glorifying the Tyrants and Oppressors

written in favour of the mass-murderers, notwithstanding the fact that they had ridiculed and fought Islam all their life, as Saddam and his fellow murderers did. These websites open the doorway-to-heaven for mass-murderers by totally ignoring numerous explicit injunctions against the oppressors in Islam's sacred Revealed Book, which also unequivocally condemns the killing of innocent souls.

Justification for Saddam ending up in the Garden of Paradise would almost certainly redouble if he should be killed by the Americans. Debauched thinking of this type has imposed on the Muslim masses since antiquity, rulers who believed that it was their holy prerogative to kill innocent people to keep themselves in power. And at the end of the day, the tale-telling would completely purify them from the guilt of every heinous crime they would have committed. When people start playing 'God', that is the beginning of the end.

As a reaction to the killing of Uday and Qusay, a lady from Egypt e-mailed one of the Arab satellite stations regretting their death and considering it as a "set-back for all Muslims". A man from Saudi Arabia wrote that although they were oppressors, they had been killed in "cold-blood". The head of the clan of Saddam told *Al Jazeerah*, on 27 July 2003 that he had demanded the corpses of the two brothers to be handed over so that they may be buried in accordance with the Islamic and tribal traditions. Why were the Islamic and tribal traditions not even worth a mention when thousands of people were being slaughtered and their families were not informed about their whereabouts or the whereabouts of their dead bodies? Did Saddam or for that matter, his clan, have any feelings that the bodies that are being brought out of the mass graves should have been handed over to their kith and kin for respectable burial? But under their subnormal logic, the Islamic and traditional and tribal values only apply to them and not to anyone else who opposes their bestiality. When people lose the faculty of balanced thinking and a sense of justice, then they invite disasters upon themselves. With these types of 'leaders', nobody needs an enemy. The supporters of Saddam are directly responsible for the tragedy that has befallen Iraq and they should be made accountable to the

Chapter 3: The Sedition of Glorifying the Tyrants and Oppressors

people of Iraq.

In order to promote their own political preconceptions, some of the Muslim organizations do not even feel a prick of conscience about lying blatantly to the public. It is essential to evaluate the mind rot that has befallen some so-called Islamic elements who would stoop to revere the oppressors, so long as they share their political ideology and their stance against the US. Needless to say, there is no objectivity in this type of approach. It is based primarily on hatred mongering. It heavily relies on guesswork and conjecture, as the case-study that follows will prove.

An anonymous author in one popular Yahoo Group has written, what he calls, an analytical article, under the title 'Why were Uday and Qusay killed?' He makes erratic allegations, which no person acquainted with Iraqi affairs could digest. But one is bound to feel sorry for misinformed people who might get innocently carried away. He writes, "the Zionist media [CNN, MSNBC, FOX, NBC, ABC, CBS] let loose a barrage of propaganda according to which, the two [Uday and Qusay] had committed 'terrible crimes' against Iraqis".

The Zionist factor, as always, has to be introduced out of place and out of context, so as to absolve the Arab and Muslim officials from the cobweb of menace they have created for themselves. The underlying message is that, as it was the Zionist media that were responsible for broadcasting their 'terrible crimes', the claim is untrustworthy. Many Muslim people, however, are quite capable of seeing farther than the tip of their nose. One may ask, what about the non-Zionist media that have broadcasted and televised programmes about remorseless vicious crimes committed by the two brothers? Their crimes were common knowledge in non-Zionist media long before their killing.

The author continues with his analysis that, one Zionist channel claimed that they had killed thousands, another that they had killed hundreds, another that they had raped and murdered, while another one said that Uday could pick up any woman he liked. Hence, he alleges that there is inconsistency and non-reliability in the accusation by the Zionist media.

Chapter 3: The Sedition of Glorifying the Tyrants and Oppressors

The matter does not concern polemics. It concerns facts of history. If the author had cared to ponder over his own inconsistent thinking, he could not have escaped coming into collision with moral and religious viewpoints. What difference does it make whether they had killed ten or one hundred or a thousand innocent souls? On the matter of principle, their crimes against humanity, together with those of their father, are well-documented and well-publicized in the non-Zionist media. If the author wants to allege that the Arab media and non-Arab Muslim media are subservient to the Zionists for having televised numerous programmes on the crimes of the two brothers, then, such an analysis cannot win any credibility even among the most naïve observers.

Then the author asks: "Why this barrage of propaganda?" He himself answers: "TV viewers often miss why the Zionists put out these stories. The obvious fact is that the murder of Saddam's sons by 200 troops is very difficult, if not impossible to defend under international law and Islamic law."

The self-appointed spokesman of international and Islamic law stands as an attorney, judge and jury, in absolute sympathy with the two brothers who had not started their career in crimes from a vacuum. They had a history of full training which they translated into their brutal and barbaric conduct, even against their own inner circle of bodyguards and secret police as well as Iraqi athletes. But the author, for the sake of anti-Americanism, misleads his readers by misconstruing the 35-year rule of the blood-stained Ba'athists in Iraq. This defence is considered justified for the evil brothers, who, never ever concealed their absolute disgust and resentment towards religious values and morality.

The author warns his readers: "Note this analysis. No one else is going to have the courage to write this." What can one make from this self-gratifying statement? It seeks to show how brilliant the author is. He has clearly ranked himself in the category of exclusive and exceptional analysts, whom no one else can match. Therefore, his analysis has to be analyzed and reviewed at length.

He writes: "The U.S. did not go into Iraq because of the behaviour of Qusay and Uday". And who says it did? The US has not

Chapter 3: The Sedition of Glorifying the Tyrants and Oppressors

claimed so either. Nor has anybody else claimed that the conduct of the two brothers was the cause of the US-led war. What is the point of stating the obvious? The point follows with further weird 'analysis'. The author writes: "There was no human rights justification claimed for the invasion".

One of the objectives of war that the US made crystal clear was 'regime change' in Iraq due to its brutality and due to its human rights violations. When the US declared its intention, there followed a controversy which was debated in America, Europe and the Arab world under the full light of the international media. It is surprising that the author has not come across a single article out of hundreds that are available in national newspapers and the internet on the goal of 'regime change' due to human rights abuses. He continues that the US has violated international law because of invasion and that it has found no weapons of mass destruction. He asserts: "So Qusay and Uday were not killed because they were 'brutal' and liked to drink and womanize. They were killed because they stood up to the U.S. and would not cooperate with the U.S." He contrasts this scenario with that of Saddam's son-in-law who was killed by Saddam because he cooperated with the CIA and leaked the secrets of the nation, according to the author.

The author simply ignores the fact that Saddam's sons had exhausted all the alternatives for saving their own skin. When all the avenues of escape were sealed and the surrender would have meant being tried for crimes against humanity, they made their last stand. Why did they not face the Americans to save Baghdad from falling? Why did the huge army and republican guards under Qusay simply abandon Baghdad, thus bringing disgrace to the honour of the Arab people? Therefore, to claim that they were killed because they stood up to the US is an insult to common sense.

The author reaches a self-contradictory conclusion. He writes: "There has been no impartial inquiry which would indicate that Qusay and Uday committed the atrocities they are accused of having committed." A passionately biased person would not recognize conventional rules of proving guilt. The author has chosen not to heed what many people around the world have become aware

Chapter 3: The Sedition of Glorifying the Tyrants and Oppressors

of. The guilt can be proved with the discovery of mass graves and eye-witness reports, which have been televised even in the non-Zionist media.

In the very next sentence, the author ironically writes: "It's quite possible that before 1991, Qusay and Uday did commit atrocities..." Who carried out an impartial inquiry on their involvement in the atrocities of 1991? There is no escape from resorting to the same conventional method of the discovery of mass graves, eye-witness reports and evidence of the victims, which determine the guilt, as in the case of Bosnia and Kosovo.

In the next sentence, the author writes: "However, under Hosni Mubarak in Egypt, torture, rape and murder are quite common against Islamic opponents of the regime. The U.S. pays Mubarak $2.8 billion every year to keep it that way." This brings us to the crux of the matter which reflects how the twisted logic nullifies the argument. If the mass-murderers happen to be anti-US, then all their crimes are justified and are to be blessed. But if the alleged crimes are committed by pro-US forces, then this is ranked as outrageous and unacceptable. So there is no principle and no moral argument involved. The author judges the commission of crimes against humanity on the basis of who is pro-US and who is anti-US.

As regards what he calls "propaganda about the lifestyles of Uday and Qusay", the author claims that "we repeatedly see Uday's cigars on TV (Cuban?) as well as Saddam's palaces." Then he offers a solution: "The propaganda seems aimed at gullible Muslims: They were corrupt, so Americans did us a favour by killing them." He continues: "These Muslims do not use their brains and think. ..."!

The allegation is based on nothing but imagination, totally divorced from objectivity. The fact is that Uday had his cigars specially made in Cuba and shipped exclusively in his name. This is documented in several videos, which the regime itself has left behind. So there is no question of 'propaganda', unless of course, the meaning of 'propaganda' has changed in the English dictionary. If the Zionist media are guilty of showing the cigars in the mouth of Uday, time and again, then the Arab media are even guiltier for showing the same scene, many more times than the American media

Chapter 3: The Sedition of Glorifying the Tyrants and Oppressors

have shown it. There is no question of propaganda in showing Saddam's palaces, which tragically, he would not be able to carry with him to his final abode.

There is no denying the fact that Saddam built luxurious palaces when his people were dying of hunger. The amounts robbed from the national treasury of Iraq for building Saddam's palaces, could have provided medicines for millions of dying children. To call it 'propaganda' is like indulging in reckless camouflage. Moreover, American officials have never claimed that just because the two brothers used to drink and womanize and were corrupt, they killed them as a favour to Muslims. This is self-imposed obsessive thinking. Thank goodness that other Muslims have refrained from using their brains in such a spurious way.

The savagery of Saddam's regime has shocked the world but not his lackeys who are still bent on abusing their status, whether as 'Islamic spokesmen' or as preachers from the pulpits. Crimes against humanity on a mammoth scale have been committed against the people of the nation and not against any foreign invaders, yet, certain imams of the mosques are totally void of any sense of justice. Times are changing. People are becoming conscious of their human rights. They will not tolerate obsolete hypotheses which preach that the unjust rulers and their sons and family members are above the law and are not accountable for any of the dreadful crimes they commit. Because of such odious thinking, the Muslim community has been victimized and is facing the most contemptible phase in its history. Due to the betrayal of the Islamic Law and Islamic concept of Justice by the imams of the rulers, the people who suffer the most are ordinary, poor, destitute and defenceless.

A candid message has to be passed to the defenders of the oppressors who consider them as 'representatives of God on earth'. The Ba'athists have left conspicuous evidence in the form of video-taped records of the monstrous corporal punishment they meted out, not only to their opponents, but also to petty offenders among the civil servants. If the blind supporters of the devils do not have eyes to see the nauseating scenes that have been televised on several TV channels, they should not assume that everybody else is blind. The way in which the inhuman regime of Saddam sought to strangulate and humiliate the human feelings and sentiments, is perhaps unmatchable in modern history. Even people in the pre-Islamic Era of Ignorance used to treat their animals and beasts better than Saddam treated human beings.

On 1 August 2003, on the eve of the thirteenth anniversary of Saddam's incursion into Kuwait, *Al-Arabiya,* an independent TV channel from Dubai, televised the first interview of Raghd, the daughter of Saddam, who, together with her sister and their nine children were given protection by the Jordanian government on humanitarian grounds. By evading an answer on Hussein Kamel, her husband, she was only prepared to say, as she put it, for the "honest record of history" that both the sons-in-law, Hussein and Saddam Kamel were extremely loyal to her father. Of course, they were loyal to their master. But the question that should have been posed was, whether Saddam and his sons-in-law were loyal to the people of Iraq.

It is the slavish loyalty of Hussein Kamel to his master that led him to supervise with all sincerity, the butchery of thousands of noble souls during the popular uprising. Thousands of families were ruined by this Saddam loyalist. When both his sons-in-law defected to Jordan, they were accused of having committed treason by leaking the state secrets to the CIA. So they were lured back into Iraq after being promised amnesty, and were killed by Saddam. The story is told in many articles published in Arabic since 1991. Yet, one of the interviewers on *Al-Arabiya* mentioned the name of Hussein Kamel by invoking God's mercy on him. For the 'honest record of history', light should have been shed on their background which was full of treachery. The interviewer on *Al-Arabiya* must have been aware of what status has been given in Islam and in the Arab culture to the treacherers.

The interview was repeated on the same channel on 9 August, but this time, *Al-Arabiya* interviewed those who were abreast of the inside stories of inter-rivalries within the ruling family. Saddam's daughter claimed that Baghdad fell because the closest aides of Saddam on whom he relied totally, betrayed him. The entire political life of Saddam is full of betrayals. After 1991, he betrayed his closest

Chapter 3: The Sedition of Glorifying the Tyrants and Oppressors

comrades in the party and installed his own clan and family members in almost all the official positions. As expected, Saddam's daughter overlooked the well-established facts of history that her father was an absolute dictator and was commander-in-chief of the armed forces. If the commander himself can run away, who can blame the army for melting away? The commander has to take the entire blame for betraying his nation, rather than passing the buck to others. His orders carried more weight than the Commands of God the Almighty, in the eyes of his immoral and corrupt officials.

Saddam's daughter particularly named Ali Hassan Al-Majeed for betrayal and cursed him twice during the interview. She blamed him for murdering Saddam's sons-in-law. She also pointed the finger at Saddam's three brothers. Raghd did not ask herself one simple question: Who appointed these corrupt officials to the top positions? Ali Hassan Al-Majeed was a taxi driver; suddenly Saddam installed him as head of intelligence. He turned the Iraqi people into prisoners in their own country, with the full consent of his boss. His only qualification was that he was Saddam's cousin. Saddam's own brothers were demoted because of a family feud and then were suddenly promoted to the top government posts.

Amir Al-Hilwoo, a writer and political analyst from Baghdad, said on the programme that the army personnel on whom Saddam depended were accustomed to taking bribes. How can such morally rotten army personnel be trusted to defend the country? Saddam gave charge to his son Qusay for the defence of Baghdad, although he had no military training or expertise, except in murdering innocent people.

Hamid Al-Bayati, the spokesman of the Islamic Revolution in Iraq laid the blame fairly and squarely on Saddam, the master of all the mischief in Iraq. Saddam's daughter herself confessed in front of millions of viewers, whilst recounting her father's 'kindness and compassion', that he had bestowed many favours to his family members by placing them in top official ranks, when they would never have progressed beyond being schoolteachers! He allotted to them agricultural lands and enriched them. Even under the ancient oppressive Byzantine Empire, these points would not have been

Chapter 3: The Sedition of Glorifying the Tyrants and Oppressors

counted as plus points. This means that Saddam considered the wealth and resources of Iraq as his family's property.

Though Raghd tried to absolve Hussein Kamel from the charge of treason, Amir Al-Hilwoo said that he was part and parcel of all the crimes committed by the regime. Both Izzaddin Al-Majeed, Saddam's cousin from London and Amir Al-Hilwoo from Baghdad, agreed on the programme that the issuance of amnesty by Saddam to his sons-in-law and the objection raised by Ali Hassan Al-Majeed on behalf of the family, was a prearranged drama, that was played in the official meeting. Al-Bayati said that the UN was on the verge of lifting the sanctions on the basis that 90 percent of Iraq's chemical and biological weapons were already destroyed. But it was Hussein Kamel's outburst in Jordan, claiming that Iraq still had weapons of mass destruction that resulted in the prolongation of sanctions. If millions of Iraqi children died as a result, it did not matter so long as his own children were safe and sound. This in itself was a flagrant betrayal of the people of Iraq.

The ex-personal secretary of Uday, Abbas Al-Janabi, while commenting on the interview of Saddam's daughter, said that Uday had looted and robbed all the possessions of his brother-in-law. He also said that if Uday were alive, his sister would not have dared to appear for a TV interview. Both Abbas Al-Janabi and Izzaddin Al-Majeed, concurred that Uday was a wicked person, whose drunken associates even terrorized their own family members. The guests on the programme reiterated that the most incompetent tribal members of Saddam were installed in very sensitive and key positions, in which they grossly abused their power. If this was not betrayal of the nation, then what was it?

Saddam's daughter pretended to be unaware that Saddam has another son called Ali from another wife, Samira Shah Bandar. The ex-secretary of Uday refuted this claim. He said that Ali was in charge of one of the most popular youth clubs in Iraq. He said that he had specific instructions from Uday to stop any praise and any mention of his brother Ali in the official press.

The bizarre trend of invoking the mercy and blessings of God on the oppressors and mass-murderers is as visible as bright sunshine

Chapter 3: The Sedition of Glorifying the Tyrants and Oppressors

in the history of Muslim nations. It may not yet have occurred to Radovan Karadzic and Ratko Mladic, the architects of genocide in Bosnia, that if they could land up in a Middle Eastern country with an assumed convert name, they too could qualify for 'mercy and blessings', if America permits. They may even win protection on humanitarian or compassionate grounds. Some clerics may choose to glorify them from their pulpits, without the least regard for the bereaved families, who would have lost their breadwinners in cold blood and would have become paupers overnight.

One simply cannot comprehend what sort of disease this is, of invoking compassion and mercy for the mass-killers, who would have thrived on their remorseless satanic career throughout their reign. To show insensitivity to the fatal plight of the aggrieved families and those exterminated through ethnic cleansing is an affront to human decency. Would any Arab or Muslim government be prepared to offer refuge on humanitarian or compassionate grounds to the women and children whose lives have been devastated and shattered because of the crimes of these evil people? Of course not, because they do not have in their veins the 'noble blood' of the ruling dynasties.

There are millions out there who have become innocent victims of this infected way of thinking which does not differentiate between the oppressors and the oppressed, between the murderers and the murdered, between the robbers and the robbed. If such confused thinking continues, then there might come a time when people will invoke God to bestow mercy and blessings on Satan. If Muslims need to know, there are almost 300 references in the Qur'an, Islam's Revealed Book, to oppression, oppressors and the oppressed. The most prominent part is the Divine Verdict against the oppressors. Yet, the widely practised hellish crime in the Arab and Muslim world today is oppression, and that too, wrapped under the garb of niceties and justified from a few popular pulpits.

When ethnic cleansing was carried out in the Balkans, the corpses did not include any disabled people. But in the mass graves excavated in Iraq, remains of disabled people with artificial limbs, as well as young university students, women and even children have

Chapter 3: The Sedition of Glorifying the Tyrants and Oppressors

been found. Dependent children were buried with their mothers who were executed. At the time when mass burial grounds were uncovered in the Balkans, almost all the Friday sermons televised from Arab countries condemned the savagery of the Serbs. Some even considered the genocide as Europe's war on Islam. As mass graves are being uncovered in Iraq, hardly any Friday sermon televised from the Arab countries has bothered to condemn the total disregard and disrespect for the sanctity of human life. The post-Iraq-war Friday sermon of Dr Sheikh Yusuf al-Qardawi from Qatar was the most notable exception and unique in its own right. It adopted a clear and very brave stance against the oppressors.

The bulk of religious awareness that reaches the grassroots is through Friday sermons. People do expect the pulpits to be used for imparting the right knowledge. They do not expect the pulpits to breach their trust and become vehicles for glorifying the tyrants and oppressors. In any case, it is most detestable on the part of the preachers, speakers, writers or journalists to find their ideals among the Muslim mass-murderers, as if human society is totally devoid of honourable people of virtuous standing.

If Muslims are slaughtered by non-Muslims, then this is taken as evidence of malice against Islam. But if Muslims are slaughtered by Muslims, the evasive excuses given to the public are that nobody is perfect, that we all commit mistakes, that mistakes have to be forgiven and forgotten, that one has to be forward-looking rather than brood about the past. This type of passive and apologetic thinking has brought disaster to Arabs and Muslims in their own countries. The rulers who abuse their power frivolously, are further encouraged to continue with their atrocities. If the public demands a change, they can easily obtain edicts from the corrupt court-clergy that this is nothing but 'rebellion'.

The victims of torture and brutalities are left with no support when values are turned upside down in favour of the rulers who demonstrate their apathy by shirking national and international law. Under such grim circumstances, people are told from the pulpits to keep on praying that may God guide the rulers towards the good and right path. What benefit did such prayers have on Saddam and his

Chapter 3: The Sedition of Glorifying the Tyrants and Oppressors

likes?

The fellow assassins of Saddam kept a full record of their ruthlessness in the form of video cassettes so that their boss could enjoy the sickening scenes in his spare time. As they shot at the prisoners, they cheered and clapped when the victims fell. The victims begged them to have mercy on them for the sake of God. They replied: "God has gone on holiday"! Saddam's men have left behind ample evidence of their moral bankruptcy. Yet, they were tolerated by most of the Muslim and Arab countries.

When people will start demanding their rights, the governments will suffer from sleepless nights and the rulers will suffer from heart attacks. Yet, it is the public that carries the key to any meaningful reform which is so long overdue in Muslim society.

4

Arab and Muslim Peoples - Victims of Internal Intrigues

IF stock is taken of the exceptional achievement of the Arab and Muslim world, one stark reality cannot escape attention. What the Arab governments have efficiently achieved in the last fifty-five years is to fight each other and to betray the Palestinian people and Palestine. What the Muslims have effectively achieved is to agree unanimously never to agree with each other. This may sound very pessimistic. But despite their rich resources and manpower, they have failed to unite on the matters threatening their own security and survival. Normally the causes for failure are ingrained in the negative attitude that revolves on from one generation to another. If people and their governments had embarked on a course of self-assessment and self-criticism, they would have broken the frame of mind which is always on the lookout for scapegoats.

People have been programmed to think in terms of conspiracy theories. Therefore, their own shortcomings are not visible to them. When something goes drastically wrong in the Arab and Muslim environment, the bogy is there to take the brunt. It is always 'colonialism' and 'outside forces' that are blamed, irrespective of the fact that the bulk of Muslim countries have been freed from the clutches of colonialism for over a generation. In many cases, the phobia of 'outside forces' is deliberately marketed to justify the tyranny that has evolved in the post-colonial era.

After the independence, the ex-colonies adopted a political outlook claiming that the circumstances in their countries were not ripe for democracy. So the only option in their deviant thinking was an outright dictatorship. Consequently, their records on civil liberties deteriorated. Some countries started implementing their twisted version of 'democracy'. Sentiments of people were misused and their

Chapter 4: Arab and Muslim Peoples – Victims of Internal Intrigues

hopes were stifled as 'presidencies' in the 'republics' became part of the personal estates and were inherited. Saddam's sons went a step ahead in planning to share in rotation the presidency that their father owned and leave it in his progeny.

Self-expression was allowed so long as it did not trespass on the absolute authority of the rulers. When anyone dared to question the wisdom of any government policy, he was branded a 'rebel'. Such a repugnant situation became an essential feature in autocracies and oligarchies. It closed all the avenues for constructive reforms. Men and women devoid of moral scruples bowed to this condition and idealized it. By doing so, they betrayed the sovereignty of their own people.

Elections were allowed as long as the contestant for presidency was a single candidate, who was returned to power with a majority of 99% votes, with 1% proviso for the 'wicked' absentees. A whole generation grew up under this political sham. Decadence in the political system reached its apex when dissidents were clamped down upon and thrown into jails. In this way, the dictatorial 'democracies' were responsible for giving birth to religious extremism in the modern world. The legitimate expression of dissident opinion was thwarted. People who demanded domestic reforms, by campaigning against official corruption, widespread bribery and open usurpation of citizens' rights, were branded as 'traitors'. Hence, the bigots contributed in creating extremism. The situation has deteriorated in Muslim countries to such an extent that in the civil war in Algeria and in the indiscriminate bombings it is impossible to know who is fighting whom, and for what purpose. It seems, senselessness is the order of the day.

In the midst of the mumbo-jumbo of global power politics, international attention is focused on the Arab and Muslim world that finds itself in a very difficult predicament. One only has to watch and observe the open-line programmes on the Arab satellite TV channels in order to sense the deep-felt wounds in the hearts of ordinary people for suffering humiliation after humiliation at the hands of the world powers and their satellite states. On the one hand, the political leadership of the Arab world is worried about its own

Chapter 4: Arab and Muslim Peoples – Victims of Internal Intrigues

future and survival in power. On the other hand, there is awareness among educated people and conscientious men and women, that rapid reforms have to be enacted to restore dignity to the Arab and Muslim world. The deficiencies of many decades have to be rectified. Human rights abuses that were shunned for many years have to be put right if further damage is to be prevented.

Human rights violations in Muslim countries have been widely reported. We, Muslims make sure that the world hears our anguish about the killings and flagrant breach of the fundamental rights of the native people under occupation in Palestine, Kashmir, Chechnya and other places. But abuses in Muslim countries are met with muted response at public and intellectual levels. Therefore, the victims of torture, arbitrary arrests, harassments, racial and ethnic cleansing have no other recourse but to turn to the international humanitarian agencies to air their grievances.

When the present day Muslim nation-states breach the rights of their minorities, we prefer to hide our heads in the sand like an ostrich, hoping that we might be able to conceal the ugly part of our human rights track record. We think in terms of 'we', 'us' and 'our'. Anything outside the ambit of self-centredness does not exist for us. The Muslim masses have been ambivalent about the agony of minority rights under the Muslim despots, in as much as the world today is ambivalent about the rights of Muslim people as a whole. The fruit that we reap can only be as good or as bad as the seed that we sow. It is the awareness of deficiency that may open the avenue for reform.

We forget that human life is inviolable. Whether one is a Muslim or a Jew, a Christian or a Hindu, an agnostic or an atheist, his or her life is invaluable simply because he or she has been created by the God whom we worship. But so long as he is not one of 'us', 'we' do not care. The passive attitude, that it is not 'our' lookout whatever happens to others, has created an unpleasant, yet, undeniable phenomenon in history that it is Muslims who have shed Muslim blood more than anybody else. The blurred sense of justice does not allow us to see the reality of 'cause and effect' in life. Instead of restraining the power-mongers for the excesses they have

Chapter 4: Arab and Muslim Peoples – Victims of Internal Intrigues

been committing, we prefer to hide ourselves in the oyster of non-involvement. Critical issues are constantly shrugged off. Many people among us shy away in condemning ignominious and disgraceful acts of terror that usurp the rights of others to live in peace and security. If anybody becomes a disgrace to the sublime principles of our religion, he has to be disowned.

The colonial powers, the Zionist and Hindu fanatics are blamed for racism against Arabs and Muslims in Palestine and Kashmir. Yet, many Muslims forget that some Muslim fanatical groups have degraded themselves to the lowest of the low level. Anyone who thinks that he or she is 'all-knowing, all-wise' is ignorant. It is ignorance that leads these elements to spread wholesome terror by targeting and murdering innocent people who are just going about their daily business. It is the evil ignorance that leads the fanatical elements to blow up people praying in the mosques and other places of worship, which are considered inviolable in Islamic Law. If the fanatics are trained by their clerics to enter the mosques of other Muslims at the exact time of Friday prayers and cause mayhem among innocent worshippers through suicide bombing, this deed in itself tells volumes that such wanton clerics have no religious commitments. To associate them with any religious ethics is tantamount to commit profanity. These groups are well-known to the government authorities. But they have support among government officials in some Muslim countries, so they are let loose in society. There is no reason at all why Islam and the Muslim community should be burdened with the liability of being identified with these fanatics.

It needs several years of exhaustive training, hard work and tremendous cost to produce an educated and professionally qualified person. But it takes a few seconds to destroy one in cold blood. If the ruling clique, anywhere in the Muslim land, has been tolerating racial and ethnic cleansing, boldly practised by fanatical groups, then they are failing in their minimal obligation of governance for safeguarding the security of life, property and honour of their own citizens. If such a gruesome situation is tolerated and the criminals keep on escaping justice, then this may mean that the government secret agencies are

Chapter 4: Arab and Muslim Peoples – Victims of Internal Intrigues

involved in promoting terror and ethnic cleansing.

Somehow the Muslim Establishment cannot see its own contribution in vigorously promoting fanaticism, self-righteous extremism and hence, terrorism. There is no such a thing as 'extremist' or 'radical' Islam. But there are certainly many Muslims who can be identified by these attributes. Some of them stop short of issuing 'green cards' for entry into Heaven. Only the 'chosen' people qualify, such as those who are prepared to condone reckless killing of innocent civilians. It is worth examining what mode of thinking fosters and stimulates extremism. One would hear many times from the pulpit in the Grand Mosque in Makkah, even as recently as during the Friday sermon of 15 August 2003 that the Prophet Muhammad prophesied that the Muslim community will divide into 73 divisions, one of them will go to Heaven and the rest will go to Hell. The Prophet did not actually identify or name which faction would be blessed for entry into Heaven. But the zealots among the clerics, in all earnestness, put words into the mouth of the Prophet to pronounce that it is the sect or School to which they belong that will reach Heaven. Without having any shame or guilt, they lie in the name of the Prophet.

The Grand Mosque in Makkah is the only spot on the face of the earth, where all the 73 divisions, if they have already transpired and materialized, are fully represented. Therefore, the platform of the Mosque should be the place which proclaims and promulgates in all sincerity the message of unity, love, compassion, peace and fraternity within the entire worldwide community. Instead, the representatives of the other 72 divisions, who would be physically present during the Friday sermon and prayers are told that only one division or sect would be qualified to go to Heaven, and the subscribers to the other Schools would burn in Hell. How much more extremist could it get than this?

By not naming the eligible School, the Prophet would have meant to encourage competition among the believers in the way of virtuous living, good deeds, piety, God-consciousness, mercy and generosity. Instead, the zealots among the clerics, through their verdict, pass a wrong message to the radicals and criminals, by

Chapter 4: Arab and Muslim Peoples – Victims of Internal Intrigues

implication, that even though they may be murderers, thieves, wicked and evil, so long as they belong to the specified sect identified by the clerics, they would qualify to enter Heaven. And even though the members of other Schools may be virtuous, pious, kind and disposed to do good, they would end up in Hell, just because they do not belong to the lucky sect. How much more radical could it get than this?

The terror gangsters, who would have heard the sole condition for entry into Heaven so frequently from their clerics, are prone to become obsessed with it. The ignorant among them take up arms against their own fellow Muslim brothers when they start playing 'God' to condemn people to Hell. They act as if they have a right to deputize for God and to decide matters on His behalf. They are not prepared to contemplate on the fundamental reality of life that human beings are susceptible to a barrage of errors and sins and that the extremists are no exception. It is this type of thinking that has brought terrorism into the heart of Islam's holiest land, so much so that the authorities are now facing a real challenge to contain it.

How is the extremism being nurtured? One more practical example would clarify the point. A few years ago, a top level official delegation from Iran was visiting Saudi Arabia for the pilgrimage, which is a guaranteed privilege for all Muslims under the Islamic Law, no matter what colour, race, language, nationality or School they belong to. On Friday, as the sermon was being conducted, the delegation entered the Grand Mosque of the Prophet in Madina and joined the congregation. The cleric changed his subject and directed his unethical accusation to the delegation, saying that their sect or School is not part of the Muslim community. The delegation just got up and walked out of the Prophet's Mosque. The cleric would have lectured many times on the life of the Prophet, who was so gentle that he never turned away even his bitterest enemies or non-believers from his presence, and was courteous and charitable towards friends and foes. In direct contravention to the traditions and the lifestyle of the Prophet, it did not bother the cleric that he was being harsh and rude to the Muslims belonging to other than his School, which he did not have any right to do. If he could not leave his hatred and ill-will

Chapter 4: Arab and Muslim Peoples – Victims of Internal Intrigues

at home, he did not have a right to stand on the pulpit of the Prophet in the first place. In all fairness to the Saudi authorities, they took immediate action by transferring that cleric to some remote area.

The story did not end there. There are some members on yahoo groups on the internet who preach that they support and aid the cleric who publicly insulted the Iranian delegation from the pulpit of the Prophet's Mosque. It does not worry them that they lack moral standing, which is considered to be the cornerstone of Islamic conduct. These are the people who believe that anybody who does not subscribe to their beliefs is entitled to be killed, and his life, property and honour is violable. In Pakistan, there are scores of clerics, some sitting in the National Assembly, who have taken up this abominable cause. Their judgemental attitude was naturally bound to explode into terrorism.

The counterparts of such negative thinking can be found in some extremist elements in American politics. These people are determined to sell the phobia to the public that America is facing an imminent threat from what they call 'Islamic terrorism', which is bent on destroying America. These radicals have their own ends and agenda to promote. If the scare is kept alive, it would be easier to obtain the consensus of the American public for further expansionist invasions. If there was an iota of truth in the contention that there are some terrorist groups among Muslims in the US who are determined to cause harm to America, then the Great Blackout of August 2003 in New York was a golden opportunity for these groups to indulge in terrorist activities under the cover of darkness. But it did not happen because the terrorist threat only exists in the phobic imagination of the radicals.

Similarly, on the other extreme, the radical clerics in Saudi Arabia have been selling the scare of the so-called 'grave worship', by accusing Schools other than theirs of worshipping graves, which they know is simply not true. Such misrepresentation of the facts has been promoted for marketing their own ideology. This means, accusing other Muslims of being polytheists. There are however Muslims who do pay respect to the Prophets and saints by visiting their places of burial. This is not equivalent to worship. There is not

Chapter 4: Arab and Muslim Peoples – Victims of Internal Intrigues

even a lunatic soul among the Muslims who worships graves. But if this scare is not kept alive in the back of the minds of simple-minded and unaware people, then the clerics would find real hardship in promoting their own brand of Islam. This does not mean to say that the Saudis and their learned moderate clerics have made no constructive contribution on the domestic and international fronts. Their vast contribution in efficiently administering and managing the two Grand Mosques in Makkah and Madina is very impressive. They have a vast potential to render positive services for the good of the Muslim and international community provided they can cut to size their radical clerics who breed on hatred-mongering.

Many intellectuals in the Muslim world have become endemically hypocritical. They treat with indifference the victims who are left to suffer the torment of terror and violence. Extremism and radicalism strikes at the root of balanced thinking. This inevitably brings disrepute to the good name of Islam. The resources of the responsible Muslim organizations and humanitarian agencies are sapped into defending the general Muslim outlook that the deeds of the extremists do not represent in any way the overall viewpoint of the peace-loving global Muslim community. In this situation, to hide behind the diplomacy of words and expressions, might be read as a sign of indifference towards Muslim radicalism. Hindu and Zionist extremists have enough decency not to kill and maim their own people. But the instigators among the Muslim fanatics have fallen below human dignity. Their problem is that even the dacoits, robbers and mass-murderers among them consider themselves to be 'representatives of God on earth'.

The grassroots have to grow up from being impressed by empty slogans. They have to revamp and reform their own thinking. They have to liberate themselves from a deficiency syndrome of blaming others for everything that goes wrong in our society. The folly of intolerance and fanaticism that has spread in the Muslim society acts like cancer. The day that we, Muslims, realize that we are the main impediment to our own progress, we will have won the fateful battle.

Prisoners of conscience were rotting in the jails of the

Chapter 4: Arab and Muslim Peoples – Victims of Internal Intrigues

Muslim dictators without trial. Hardcore political criminals wore two different masks – one for public display and the other for terrorizing their opponents. The victims were being gunned down by snipers on the streets of major cities in Pakistan, Afghanistan and Algeria, for no other reason than daring to have different opinions or subscribing to different beliefs. At a time when the world was banging its head on brick walls and grieving over the statues of Buddha, there was no one to lift a finger over the Mazar-e-Sharif massacre and ethnic cleansing perpetrated by the Taliban. Within a few years, that same spot became a scene of massacre of the Taliban by the American troops.

The Taliban's war with the statues of Buddha was political. They themselves made no secret of the fact that it was in reaction to the sanctions imposed by the United Nations. Otherwise, the people of Afghanistan had had no problem with the statues for the last fourteen hundred years, ever since they embraced Islam. Why all of a sudden did they realize that idol worship was strictly prohibited in Islam? And who among the Afghan Muslims worshipped Buddha anyway? Still, the United Nations and more than anybody else, the Muslim nations, did not give a fraction of the attention to the mass massacre of human souls by the Taliban as they gave to preserving the sanctity of the soul-less stones. Such is the sense of proportion and justice in the 'enlightened' Muslim countries.

People normally become conscious of terrorism when it lands on their own doorstep. In reaction to the vicious and deplorable Riyadh bombing on 13 May 2003, Prince Talal Ibn Abdul Aziz told *Al-Jazeerah* that terrorism would continue so long as there is injustice in the world. Terrorism raises its ugly head as a reaction to a number of serious issues which have been pushed under the carpet for many years. It was and is a tragic state of affairs that the Muslim community which boasts of a comprehensive religious guidance and a strict code of law against injustice and the killing of innocent souls, failed to apply these laws to itself. A bad name was given to Islam by no other than the Muslims, as if the Divine Law had condoned oppression and had demeaned human life.

Dr Idi Amin Dada, the dictator of Uganda who had been

Chapter 4: Arab and Muslim Peoples – Victims of Internal Intrigues

trained by the Israelis as a soldier, was responsible for the murder of a quarter of a million people. Eventually he found a safe abode in Islam's sacred land. If Saddam had accepted the gracious offer of asylum, he would have been his next-door neighbour, with memories to share. After the death of Idi Amin, two thousand mourners gathered in a memorial service in Uganda to honour the dictator. Those who have been perturbed by Saddam's downfall and have lost advantageous positions are likely to mourn over him for as long as they live. The 'patriot' permitted them to rob and smuggle the nation's wealth out of the country. The Jordanian government, a previous ally of the dictator, has lately frozen $500 million in its banks, which the members of the Saddam regime had deposited in their names. This explains why they were prepared to stand by the tyrant throughout his reign.

All the revealed religions have emphasized the sanctity of human life. Yet, those who are not capable of even creating the excrement of a dung-fly, indulge in vicious bloodbath to destroy human life which is the most marvelous in God's creation. They justify their bloodthirstiness under the pretext of fighting 'rebellion'. Their own rebellion, starting from grapping the power against the will of the people, and ending in treachery against human values and national interest, is neither visible nor legible to them and their supporters. There have to be mandatory rules in force, where it becomes impossible for the mass-murderers to find safe haven and to get away with their crimes against humanity. The 'mob' mentality that lingers in the Arab and Muslim culture has destructive effects for enduring two types of tyrannies. The first is the tyranny of religious fanatics who are prepared to murder, maim and plunder for political ends. The second is the tyranny of the rulers who bestow upon themselves a divine right to shape the destiny of their subjects. In the process, they create a cult around themselves by exploiting the sentiments and emotions of simple-minded people. The extreme case in the modern world was that of Saddam. At a time when his barbarity was exposed, he enjoyed the whole-hearted support of many scholars and men of religion, who considered obedience to him as incumbent upon them.

Chapter 4: Arab and Muslim Peoples – Victims of Internal Intrigues

Saddam built hegemony over the public and impressed many people in the Arab world by wasting the wealth of his nation to promote his own godfather image. He littered the country with his gigantic portraits and idols, which influenced many ill-informed people. These people felt his presence everywhere, even in mosques! One would have been disgusted to notice his portraits hanging in the direction of prayers in some mosques in Baghdad. This would have led many worshippers to feel a lump in their throats. This situation had an impact on the subconscious of many immature youths in Iraq.

On 26 March 2003 Channel 4 TV, whilst covering the 'War in Iraq', showed an angry and defiant young Iraqi man. He declared that the British and Americans would not be able to defeat the Iraqi army because, as he put it, "we believe in God, we believe in Allah". "And do you believe in Saddam Hussein?" the reporter asked. The youth replied: "Yes, Saddam Hussein like the god, Saddam Hussein like the god"! The hysterical outburst of this young Iraqi was captured and capitalized by the media and was shown on other channels as well. But the fact remains that this young man and many like him would not have known any other political system apart from Arab Socialist Ba'athism. The rulers can only be as good as the people who elect them. But what happens when people are never given a right to elect their leaders? This young man would have believed, like many in the Muslim world, that to follow any leader who grabs power with whatever repressive measures and with whatever pretensions and illegitimacy, is a sacred duty.

Muslim countries are full of contradictions. Some political parties that claim that they represent Islamic views are least concerned about Islamic values. These parties differ from each other in form and shape, in thoughts and feelings, and in words and deeds, not to mention in their style of wearing beards and multi-coloured turbans. In a rally on 28 July 2003, protesting against President Musharraf's presidency which was acquired without democratic process and without election, the supporters of Islamic parties carried the portraits of Saddam. This means that if President Musharraf was not elected, it posed a very serious matter for Pakistan. But if Saddam was not elected and never believed in anything called

Chapter 4: Arab and Muslim Peoples – Victims of Internal Intrigues

'democracy', it was perfectly acceptable for Iraq. People in the streets are victimized through deceptive manoeuvre.

In Cairo, during the war on Iraq, demonstrators were allowed to protest within the precincts of Al-Azhar mosque. Every Friday after prayers, they shouted their heads off for two to three hours, until they became tired. Then they went home and forgot all about war until the following Friday. This method was quite acceptable to the authorities. What more proof did the West want than that democracy has been well accommodated and catered for within the autocratic system? If democracy was a human being, he or she would have preferred instead, to be beheaded, mummified and laid to rest next to Tutankhamen, the Pharaoh who is said to have believed in some democratic values.

One has to learn from past mistakes, provided there is no manipulative attempt to vindicate serious crimes under the garb of mistakes. Had the Arab world and the Arab League been vigilant against supporting repressive and oppressive regimes, they would have devised a mandatory code of civilized conduct. If the Arab League had been prudent in guarding its own reputation and the interest of its member states, it would have made absolutely sure that the tyrannical conduct of the rulers remained in check and under control. With his pathetic human rights record, Saddam was tolerated by the Arab League. At the very least, after the massacre of Halabjah, he should have been kicked out of the Arab fraternity. The ghost of the Saddam regime will keep on hounding the conscience of those who did not take a stance against him, for years to come. He would not have turned into the monster that he became, had it not been for their wholehearted moral support. The man was drowned in the innocent blood of his own countrymen. Yet, certain Arab governments had rallied behind him. They share the blame for all the chaos and tumultuous circumstances that have afflicted Iraq.

The end result was very humiliating for Arab Nationalism as a whole. It turned out that one of the mightiest armies in the Arab world was, after all, only meant to serve and protect the power base of the tyrant and not the country. There are many lessons to be learnt from the tragic plight of Iraq. When too much power is concentrated

Chapter 4: Arab and Muslim Peoples – Victims of Internal Intrigues

in the hands of the handpicked few, the whole machinery of the State remains at their mercy, to be used and misused for personal and tribal benefits. In Takrit, those who lost their favourable position of the last 35 years came out with their street boys to shout: "With soul and blood, we sacrifice (ourselves) for you O Saddam" on the 66th birthday of the dictator, in absentia. Despite the fact that it had already transpired that he and his ministers, his army commanders and his republican guards betrayed Iraq to save their own lives, there would always be some people who would adore him. Only hours before the war started, Saddam and his family members robbed the Central bank of $900 million and fled, as disclosed after the war. But the enslaved mentality that he left behind in some sectors of the community, would keep on craving for him.

The negative and passive attitude that has been cultivated in the minds of the grassroots has affected the community as termites affect a tree stump. The total conviction of the public was sought throughout the centuries, by preaching that it is an obligatory duty to obey a ruler even if he is a dangerous schizophrenic. The ruler and his cronies openly deceive the public, yet the public tends to rely on their version of events. The psyche of the uninformed people in the Arab and Muslim world has been corrupted to such an extent that even if the ruler and his henchmen were to vomit, people would tend to think that they are talking philosophy, to use the expression of a political thinker.

On 27 June 2003, *Al-Arabiya* TV screened an interview with the ex-Minister of Information of Iraq, Mohammad Saeed al-Sahhaf, who since then has been given asylum in Abu Dhabi. Through his pack of lies and disinformation during the war, Sahhaf became the last link between the doomed regime of his boss and the rest of the world. President Bush said that when they told him, "the fellow" was doing his brief on the TV, he left the meetings to listen to him. As the American tanks were rolling into Baghdad, Sahhaf told the public and the press that the Americans were being badly defeated and were committing suicide at the walls of Baghdad. He was obedient to his boss by using his silly statements, which predicted the outcome of the invaders long before the war started. After the

Chapter 4: Arab and Muslim Peoples – Victims of Internal Intrigues

war, Sahhaf became a comical figure when electronic toys bearing his picture and voice sold like hot cakes in America. The outcome of the war proved conclusively how Sahhaf had misled the public with his farcical statements and briefings. Some people on the Arab streets believed that he was a patriotic hero, as shown in the same documentary on *Al-Arabiya*.

Sahhaf was given another opportunity to insult the intelligence of the public by evading answers to almost all the questions put to him by the interviewer of *Al-Arabiya*. The only information he was prepared to disclose was that he was going to write about the events leading to the fall of Baghdad. Until then, time has to stop ticking. History should cease to be written. People will have to wait patiently for Sahhaf to do his homework diligently this time. Sahhaf, who was the pillar of the propaganda machinery of the tyrant, was not repentant for his stance. Were there any regrets? None at all, otherwise, how could he have courageously surrendered himself to the Americans and got released after questioning? Were there mistakes committed by the authorities of whom he had been a part? His answer was, leave it to history. Tell us about your career, the interviewer enquired. The answer was, "this is not relevant". The Arabs are in a state of shock. What went so drastically wrong? The answer was, leave it to history.

The veteran writer and thinker, Ghassan Twaini was asked to comment on this interview on *Al-Arabiya*. He expressed the reality of the matter eloquently and pragmatically. Neither would time stop ticking, nor would history stop being written, nor would the people stop asking and inquiring about the ways the Ba'athist reign had betrayed them. People were starved and deprived of their fundamental rights as the rulers were engaged in building palaces and wasting the wealth of their nations, as is now happening in the Arab world, Twaini stressed.

History is already being written with the discovery of mass graves in the North, South and Centre of Iraq. The slaughter carried out by one of the most barbarous regimes in modern times has brought disgrace to human history. Sahhaf would be naïve to ignore these facts in his memoirs.

Chapter 4: Arab and Muslim Peoples – Victims of Internal Intrigues

The measures of repression, suppression and oppression that brought down mighty empires and civilizations and were repeated by Saddam had been showing signs of his imminent downfall. Those who sang his praise and eulogized him, and stopped short of bowing to his idols, must have been blind at heart to ignore these signs. There is a world of lessons to be learnt from the rise and fall of the dictator. However, there are those who preferred, and still prefer to remain oblivious by deceiving themselves in supporting his doomed reign. He himself and his savage cousin Ali Hassan Al-Majeed never denied that they massacred the Iraqis in the North and the South. Yet, there are some reckless people who campaign on the internet that it is unlikely that he had gassed his own people.

Much more dangerous and diabolical than physical slavery is ideological slavery. It impairs the intelligence of even those who perceive themselves to be cultured, educated and intellectuals. It is this type of slavery that filled the Arab and Muslim world with hundreds of –isms. The tyrants, under foreign ideological servitude, cannot operate in solitude. They are normally surrounded by their supporters who aid and encourage them to borrow strange ideologies and impose their brutal rule over their own people. The treacherous pens and tongues of these intellectuals who auction their honour for material gain, take a major part of the blame for abetting vicious crimes against humanity.

Amru Moosa, the Secretary-General of the Arab League said in his interview on *Al-Jazeerah* on 22 May 2003 that the discovery of mass graves in Iraq was "unacceptable" in relation to the rights of the Iraqi people. His carefully worded condemnation came thirteen years too late. After the Gulf War, the disappearance of Iraqi citizens and Kuwaiti prisoners was widely reported. But his predecessors did not have the courtesy to call for an independent international inquiry.

It is worth referring to the Human Rights Annual Report 2001 of the Foreign and Commonwealth Office in London which specifies how Saddam's son Uday ordered political execution by sword, "including gouging of eyes". Those convicted of slandering Saddam had their tongue removed. (p. 13). Can the members of the Ba'athist party honestly claim that they were not aware of how the tyrant's son

Chapter 4: Arab and Muslim Peoples – Victims of Internal Intrigues

operated in their name?

Were not the Arab governments aware of the genocide in Iraq when people fleeing in thousands carried eye-witness reports with them? Not only the lives of those who were massacred, but the lives of the blood relatives they left behind, have been completely shattered and devastated. Have the leaders bothered to see the distressing scenes of the aged mothers weeping and wailing while picking up the remains of their young ones from the mass graves? Have they heard the painful cry of the old mother who says she does not want anything in life; she only wants her son back? What a loss of dignity it was for those who chose to maintain silence in the wake of humanitarian calamity, and for what? For keeping a monster and his criminal aides in power! At the time when the Palestinian mothers are crying over the terror caused by Sharon against their children and youths, the atrocities of Saddam are uncovered day by day. Yet, Sharon would never ever dream of killing Jews. Do the Palestinian supporters of Saddam, the butcher of Iraq, get the message?

A caller to *Al-Jazeerah* on its open-line programme 'For Women only' in May 2003 emphatically claimed that what Saddam had done for the progress of Iraqi and Arab women in general, no other system had ever done. Only basic human decency was needed from Saddam's 'liberated' women to show some sensitivity and respect for the feelings of mothers, sisters, wives and daughters who had lost their closest relatives in mass-massacres. It was women, who were the prime victims of the cruelty of this fiend. It was in Saddam's torture chambers that women were raped and children were killed in front of their mothers. The documentaries shown on Abu Dhabi TV during July 2003 prove that women were being lashed and beaten in prisons by Saddam's secret police. Video clips show how prisoners were kicked in the face with heavy boots by Saddam's cowards, called republican guards. This tyrant, who was a stain on the honour of every respectable Arab, broke all the records of cruelty.

Some civility and humanitarian gesture would have gone a long way in acknowledging the pain of the bereaved women whose loved ones had been dumped in mass graves. The discovery of their dismembered bodies has created a nightmare not only for their relatives on the site, but also for those watching the scenes thousands of miles away on their TV screens. No wonder, when men or women are callous to the torment of other fellow human beings, dictators like Saddam are imposed on them.

If the 'liberated' women of Saddam feel indebted to this devil, then they have to go no farther than watch in the comfort of their homes the nauseating scenes of dreadful massacres committed by him and his party members. Since his downfall, there have been expository programmes on his fascism on the satellite channels, especially on *Al-Jazeerah, Al-Arabiya, ANN, Abu Dhabi TV* and *Al-Alam*. Abu Dhabi's channel showed an exclusive video clip of the tape obtained from inside Iraq on its evening news bulletin on 2 July 2003. The scene on the tape pertained to the punishment meted out to the traffic policemen for the 'crime' of not being present at the designated spot when the Minister of the Interior, the brother of Saddam, arrived. On Presidential orders, their hands were tied around the trunks of trees and they were lashed and kicked by three persons, across their head, face and bare body. The sons of 'liberated' women rejoiced at the scene as the traffic policemen screamed and cried in pain until they collapsed. One wonders, what type of generation did these 'liberated' women care to bring up under Saddam's patronage?

Video footages in BBC's *Reporters* programme in July 2003, showed horrendous scenes of corporal punishment which was a norm under the dictator. The purpose was to destroy and annihilate the human dignity of his victims.

Every member of human society, whose thoughts are not adulterated with venom, would sympathize with other fellow human beings, who lost their loved ones as a result of outrageous crimes against humanity. If not, then one might try imagining one's own father, brother, husband or son coming out in the form of skeletons and bones from mass graves that Saddam has left as a bequest for Arab Nationalism to loathe forever. Saddam's barbarity of summarily executing thousands without trial, provides tangible

Chapter 4: Arab and Muslim Peoples – Victims of Internal Intrigues

evidence of his ghastly crimes, except to those who would rather remain blindfolded under the guise of bigotry.

Up until the invasion of Kuwait, the tyrant enjoyed cordial relations with the UK, the US, Russia and France. These members of the Security Council must have known about the grave crimes that had become the second nature of the Ba'athists. The genocide against the people of the South of Iraq and the Kurds was widely reported by the Western media, but the governments chose to maintain the *status quo*.

Concrete humanitarian measures are long overdue in the Arab world. Drastic legal and political safeguards have to be implemented by the Arab and Muslim nations to ensure that no other Saddam is ever tolerated under any circumstances. The sadistic tyrant and his satanic party must be the last to raise their obnoxious heads in the Arab world. At the same time, there has to be a thorough investigation into the crimes and finances of the Ba'ath party officials. Saddam could not have built his evil reign without their wholehearted support. They supplied foundation stones for the discredited system, without giving a second thought to the future of their own children and dependants. The wealth that was smuggled out of the country has to be frozen and handed over to Iraq. Trials must be held and those found guilty of crimes against humanity must be punished, so that justice may prevail without any partiality. This would convey a loud message to the rulers that the modern world will not tolerate any bestiality in their conduct. They cannot expect to hold on to power by divorcing humanity from their actions and manners.

5

Human Rights and Human Wrongs

THE most widely discussed concept in the present world is Human Rights. It affects us at every phase of life. Humanitarian Laws, charters, covenants and treaties give much importance to the basic freedom and fundamental rights of individuals. But their enforceability drastically differs from one region to another and from one culture to another. In some parts of the world, human rights abuses are borne by the poor, destitute and illiterate.

Human Rights, whether seen from religious or secular perspectives, tend to serve some moral objectives. They emanate from a serious concern in human society that the rights of people to live in peace and security must be safeguarded. Therefore, proper checks and controls have to be in place to limit the power of the State from infringing the rights of its own citizens and of other people. The abuse may be caused by a combination of political, social and economic factors or by sheer arrogance and pride.

Protective measures incorporated in religious scriptures and international legal documents purport to act as deterrent to exploitation. International protocols urge the signatories among the member states to include human rights provisions in their laws, so that accountability can be maintained. But despite all the emphases, human rights for the majority of the inhabitants of the world are in limbo.

The First World War ended with a startling declaration by the Allied and Associated Powers. It was declared that the war was "the greatest crime against humanity and [against] the freedom of peoples that any nation calling itself civilized has ever consciously committed ..."[33] In the First World War, ten million people were killed. In the Second World War, 55 million people were killed. On 6 August 1945, Hiroshima was destroyed. The bomb used on

Chapter 5: Human Rights and Human Wrongs

Hiroshima was developed under a secret project in which "100,000 workers took years to bring to completion".[34] Three days later on 9 August, President Truman destroyed Nagasaki with an atomic bomb in which 70,000 people perished. He warned that more atomic bombs would be dropped, and threatened "a rain of ruin from the air, the like of which has never been seen on this earth". Four hours after the explosion, nothing could be seen in the city. "The wonder weapon", as it was called, created by British and American scientists, was described as "the greatest scientific discovery in history".[35]

The author of the paper titled 'CTBT – A Psychological Profile' observes that if Hiroshima and Nagasaki had been European instead of Asian towns, they would never have been used as "guinea-pigs for massive human-killing-experiment". Many years later, when the Smithsonian Institute in Washington DC planned to hold an exhibition of the effects of Hiroshima and Nagasaki, the Congress did not give its consent. The exhibition was considered as an attack on America, "which mean nothing less than America is always right", writes Edward Said.[36]

Members of the United Nations felt that as mankind had passed through untold sorrows, it was time to reaffirm fundamental human rights. These were intended to be based on justice and respect, tolerance and promotion, economic and social advancement, of all peoples.[37]

The United Nations Declaration of Human Rights was passed on 10 December 1948, in line with its charter of existence, which was, "to maintain international peace and security" and "the sovereignty and equality of its members."[38]

For the first time, it was acknowledged in an international legal document that human beings are born free and equal in dignity and rights. (Article I). The entitlement to rights and freedoms is to be without distinction of race, colour, sex, language, religion, status or political opinion. (Article II). Everyone has the right to life, liberty and security. (Article III). No one shall be held in slavery or servitude. (Article IV). The Declaration comprises thirty articles with numerous sub-sections.

This was followed by different Conventions – for example,

Chapter 5: Human Rights and Human Wrongs

the granting of independence to colonial countries, spelling out the rights of refugees and stateless persons, the rights of women to vote, the elimination of discrimination against women and the rights of children. All types of exploitation and suppression were categorically outlawed. The right of labour to a fair wage was preserved. Civil and political rights were covered in great detail in the Conventions and preambles.

The importance of acquiring education has been covered by Clause A26 of the Universal Declaration of Human Rights which states: "Everyone has the right to education". This is a noble statement, but the UN has yet to devise mandatory mechanisms for enforcing this provision on its member nations. Lack of education or no education in some parts of the world, is one of the instruments of inequity, which widens the gap between rich and poor. In poor countries, higher education is considered a luxury that only the rich can afford.

The problems of poverty encountered by some developing nations have many dimensions. The political system itself, in many cases, inhibits the development of institutions of higher education, despite the fact that this may be a vital channel for tackling underdevelopment. Many 'Third World' countries face a shortage of skilled workers. Their educated class prefers to immigrate to the developed world because of political strangleholds and tortuous bureaucracy.

The developing nations suffer from 'brain-drain', which means a shortage of clever, skilled and educated people, arising from migration from country of origin to a foreign land. The fate of many educated and skilled people is severely limited because the politicians have created artificial immobility of labour. Even when this barrier is removed, ability and merit are not considered priority factors for providing employment opportunities. There are many talented and educated people who cannot improve their standards of living because promotion in their countries is based on the links and connections with influential figures. This amoral attitude acts as a contributory factor to the stagnation of development of human skills and resources thus contributing towards poverty.

Chapter 5: Human Rights and Human Wrongs

In heavily populated developing countries, talented graduates seeking admission into reputable universities are unlikely to gain admission if they cannot afford to give a donation to the university. How much of this donation goes to the university itself and how much of it ends up in the coffers of the politicians sitting on the Board of Governors cannot be determined. The process remains off-record. Courteous and kind terminology is attributed to what is essentially a bribe. Sometimes it is called a 'donation' and sometimes a 'contribution'. Hence, many bright students of poor and 'low caste' families are deprived of a decent education. Foreign students, especially from rich countries, are favoured over the native candidates. The reason is that they can easily afford to pay a donation of as much as 14-15 hundred thousand rupees which, when converted into US dollars, is far less than the annual fees the students might have to pay back home. Apart from other direct costs, students seeking admission into say, a medical university abroad, believe that they are spared the stringent entry requirements for limited places in the Western universities.

In India the price for admission into a good medical university increases as the politicians struggle to match supply with demand. Domestic talent suffers due to short-term gains. The nation is left with a shortage of skilled and educated people. In the rural areas, people live below the poverty line. The corrupt among the politicians strictly operate on the basis of 'make hay while the sun shines'. For the 'low caste', the slogan of equal opportunity is a myth. This matter has attracted widespread scrutiny in the Indian press. Influence peddling is very common, leading to downright discrimination that bars progress on the basis of merit. Actions aimed at promoting self-interest result in negative repercussions on human life. Human abilities are misused, maligned and misdirected for the benefit of the influential overlords in society. Nepotism, favouritism and corruption, act as cancerous cells in the developing societies. To make things worse, bureaucracy takes its toll on restraining the development of human resource - the most valuable of all the resources. Meaningless bureaucracy reflects the mental complex from which the bureaucrats suffer. Protracted bureaucratic

Chapter 5: Human Rights and Human Wrongs

procedures indicate the lack of self-confidence on the part of the bureaucrats. Bureaucracy makes life difficult for the people and makes them feel as if life is burdensome. Whereas life is the most beautiful bounty one could enjoy.

It would be a tragedy if the religious environment, anywhere in the world, becomes vulnerable to the same epidemic from which the secular environment suffers. Nevertheless, a trend is developing whereby we, Muslims, are failing to represent ourselves even on a religious forum, on a common goal and united basis. Everyone likes to run the show in his own way. Those who should be the exemplars and role models of unity are least concerned about these values. We fail to realize our true potential because of intolerance, bigotry and perceptible discrimination against each other within our own ranks. We remain out of touch with our own selves. Unfortunately, some religious organizations are capable of ruthlessly crushing the talents and potential in the community to please and satisfy political manoeuvreing in the name of religion, or the pride and egoism of those who are in a position of trust. Yet, they like to discharge the trust according to their own whims and prejudices. What about the sense of justice? Sense of justice is a utopia that is best deferred to an unforeseeable future. Such is the prevailing attitude that creates barriers in the way of talents. But after all, this is our internal problem. Its solution, therefore, has to be sought from within. Escapism from reality is not a solution.

There is a vast area of potential for the promotion of education and equity that remains unexplored. Muslims and other communities would be failing in their duty if their allegiance does not fall, first and foremost, towards humanity, peace and justice and co-existence with people of other races and religions. Many Jews, Christians, Hindus and people of various faiths are peace-loving. They are not war-mongering. They are as concerned as Muslims are for the protection and preservation of human life on earth from man-made disasters, hostilities, wars, diseases, poverty, starvation and the monopolization of education. Muslims can join hands with these peace-loving Jews, Christians, Hindus and people of other denominations to serve common causes. In the West, tremendous

Chapter 5: Human Rights and Human Wrongs

constructive and productive work has been done in this field at the national and international level by the Council of American-Islamic Relations, the Muslim Council of Britain, the Islamic Foundation, the Islamic Human Rights Commission and other dedicated organizations. The grassroots have to be made aware of their dormant prowess that can be mobilized in promoting peace and justice.

The latent potential of the masses can be realized by Muslims worldwide in raising the standards of education, discipline, the promotion of knowledge, tolerance and spirit of co-existence. Muslims cannot expect international community and people of other faiths to join hands with them in pursuit of noble causes for the welfare of humankind, if they themselves remain divided. Our capabilities can be accomplished through unity, mutual respect and tolerance and not through fanaticism and intolerance. The greatest honour that the Muslims can claim with other communities is through devotional and sincere service for the benefit of others and not through the humiliating servitude to the international warlords.

The extremists and radicals among Muslims would have to take inventory of their abominable actions and the extent of damage they have inflicted on themselves and on the community at large. No cause can possibly be served by killing innocent people. The poor Africans who were killed in cold blood in the US embassy bombings in Kenya and Tanzania had families to maintain and feed. Suddenly their children and dependants were left in destitution. Killing of one bread winner means murdering the entire dependent household.

But there are other drawbacks too that cannot be underestimated. For instance, in oil-rich countries, there is a very high unemployment rate even among graduates. If equal opportunities were available, the main criteria for promotion and progress would be merit and hard work. But in practice, opportunities are based on nepotism and influence-peddling. Unemployment in the countries that are not welfare states, causes negative and destructive reaction, leading the youth to other subversive activities.

In addition to education and employment opportunities, acute problems of hunger and starvation need to be tackled at a global level. But political considerations hinder the efforts of humanitarian organizations. The United Nations passed the International Covenant on Economic, Social and Cultural Rights under General Assembly resolution No. 2200A (XXl) on 16 December 1966. Paragraph A11 reads: "The States Parties of the present Covenant, recognizing the fundamental right of everyone to be free from hunger, shall take, individually and through international co-operation, the measures, including specific programmes." On the basis of this provision, the UN should have embarked on a soul-searching exercise. Had it done so, it would have found violations of its own rules within its precincts, engineered by the powerful nations. The most recent violations of Humanitarian Law were the sanctions on Iraq, which were aggravating the problem of hunger in that country.

The crucial problem of hunger in Africa and reparation for slave labour has been widely discussed in international forums. There were a number of related and highly contested issues that were included in the agenda of the International Conference on Racism. The African countries, comprising 53 members, submitted proposals to the UN preparatory meetings for the World Conference against Racism, Racial Discrimination, Xenophobia and Related Intolerance, held from 31 August to 8 September 2001 in South Africa. They intended to pursue their demand for compensation for the inhuman practice of slavery, the institution that starved and tortured people for the benefit of the extorters.

Amnesty International in its introduction on 'Racism and the administration of justice' observes that racism is linked to "broad economic and social issues" and to the "modern globalized market economy". These factors have given rise to what it calls, "dominant groups" over the "poor and the marginalized", who have been faced with "exploitation, oppression and discrimination" for many generations. Racial groups of the deprived class are considered "biologically inferior" and therefore, they are "enslaved, impoverished and disenfranchised or even exterminated", to use Amnesty's expressions. This discrimination which purports to create inequality among human beings succeeds in "blocking access to

Chapter 5: Human Rights and Human Wrongs

education, land and resources, jobs, positions of influence and prosperity".

In a nutshell, Amnesty has highlighted the causes, which have plagued human society in many parts of the world. The widening gulf between rich and poor has resulted in extreme poverty. The flamboyant cities of America and their lifestyle provide an image of fantasy to the poor villagers of Africa. The globalization of the economy has failed badly to bridge the gap between the affluent and poor countries and to solve the global crisis of hunger and poverty.

Globalization has imposed many humanitarian problems on poor nations on behalf of transnational corporations. Sometimes, the developing countries act as dumping grounds for toxic chemical waste. The developed world is vigilant not to risk the health of its own citizens by disposing of its industrial waste around its shores. Therefore, agreement is obtained from countries with autocratic governments for allowing the toxic waste of the West to be offloaded on their shores and land. If diseases were to spread in the developing world, the unrepresentative governments who are not accountable to their own people anyway, would not face any inquiry, and the public outcry can easily be muted and subdued.

Health hazards caused by pollution have become an issue of international concern and have been debated from all the conceivable angles by the environmentalists. Pollution is caused by the waste and garbage produced by man and not by nature. Toxic chemical and industrial waste pollutes riverbeds from where sand and gravel are excavated for the manufacture of building materials. One of the most harmful ingredients in air pollution is caused by smoke from petroleum products, with a greater danger to densely populated cities. Insecticide and fungal diseases affect crops and wildlife.

In the West, governments do take measures to control the use and disposal of chemical and toxic materials, and pesticide and insecticide on farms, in order to protect environmental health and the life of other species. This is done through laws, regulations, and supervision by Ministry of Environment agencies. Issues that have

Chapter 5: Human Rights and Human Wrongs

been debated on common platforms by the international community are the greenhouse effect, global warming and the rise in the level of the ocean. This causes flooding, with tremendous loss to crops and damage to cultivable land and residential properties.

On the crisis of global warming, Raymond Bradley, director of the University of Massachusetts's Climate System Research Centre said that, "...we have good, strong scientific evidence supported by the vast majority of scientists who ...say we are facing a serious problem". He was speaking at a Conference hosted by the Desert Research Institute. Further scientific findings presented at the Conference indicated that since 1950, major floods were attributable to global warming. Researchers expressed their contempt that the Bush Administration had chosen to take only voluntary and not mandatory measures to combat such a dangerous threat from greenhouse-gas emissions.[39]

Damage to the ozone layer, ultraviolet radiation and danger to the living organisms on earth, have also attracted much attention in recent years. Perhaps, the greatest risk to human life is the uncontrolled use of pesticides and the disposal of radioactive wastes from nuclear power stations.

Some ex-colonies are also used as junkyards for consumable goods, which have outlived their useful life. Because of health inspections and consumer protection afforded to citizens in the developed countries, expired items are removed from the shelves due to fear of incurring fines. But these products end up in countries that are totally unaware of health issues, and are still lagging behind as a result of lack of education and poverty.

In Mauritania, for example, civil war and animosity between rival tribes continued under French fomentation. The country has become, according to Kevin Bales, "dumping ground for European goods that have passed their 'sell by dates' "[40] He writes that medicines available in the pharmacies show expiry dates and yet, they are sold to the patients without any supervision. This is the price the Mauritanians are paying for their high illiteracy rate.

To divert attention from the real issues that need to be tackled to alleviate world poverty, powerful media campaigns

Chapter 5: Human Rights and Human Wrongs

promoted by interest groups, go on to blame 'over population' as the main cause of poverty. Many countries, rich in resources, are in fact under populated. What is conveniently forgotten is that the so-called over populated countries are afflicted with the worst record of corruption practised by feudalists, industrialists and politicians. In many of these countries, the lifestyle adopted by the ruling class betrays the extravagant, wasteful and luxurious lifestyle of the ancient emperors. The Byzantine emperors would have been shocked had they noticed the hedonism of the present-day totalitarian rulers.

Many poor nations face savage repression at the hands of megalomaniacs who are not prepared to abandon, at any cost, the luxuries afforded by illicit power and wealth. In these countries, people and their leaders live in two different worlds. Poor allocation and mal-distribution of national wealth, and not 'over population' are responsible for robbing the poor families of education and compelling them to live in poverty below the subsistence level. The whole set-up is artificial and man-made, with total disregard for the human life and its needs.

India is very rich in human, land and mineral resources. The poverty in the country has no bearing on its rocketing population rate. In Mumbai, where the rate per square foot of land is the highest in the world, the city is expanding vertically by leaps and bounds. Where people can afford to pay millions of rupees for a small flat in the towering building structures, the footpaths of the city are full of poor people in rags who live, marry, produce children and die on the streets. This is a common scenario in the congested major cities of India, not because there is a lack of land, but because there is a poor allocation of land which aggravates poverty. In contrast, India also houses the most beautiful, flamboyant, residential structures. India is the largest democracy in the world. It also hosts the largest disparity between rich and poor. It is a democratic right of the rich to become richer and of the poor to become poorer, except that the poor do not have control over their conditions. It is imposed on them by those who monopolize the resources of the nation.

No wonder that in such a huge country, the eccentric

situation of starvation occurs in villages which are supposed to be agriculture-intensive. The poor are exploited at the hands of the industrialists in the urban areas and at the hands of the feudalists in the rural areas. The 'low-caste' and 'high-caste' division is a tangible reality in Indian society. Whether in relation to the acquiring of education or deriving a better standard of living, the 'low-castes' are discriminated against as a way of life. A 'high-class' Brahmin would never dream of living on the streets with his children. But this condition is considered a norm for the 'low-caste' or 'untouchables' as they are called. The Indian leader Gandhi started his revolution to combat the inhuman discrimination against the 'untouchables', but the cruel victimization and segregation in Indian society survived because only the effects of the age-old problem were tackled, and not the causes.

Apart from very complex religious factors, the avarice of the moneylenders ties the downtrodden into the never-ending cobweb of exorbitant interest on personal loans. The corrupt politicians exploit the sentiments of the illiterate by playing the card of religion and race. The impact of exploitation by the elites has been in force long before the foreigners set foot on Indian soil, and it is continuing long after the foreigners have left Indian soil.

Kevin Bales writes: "Debt against which a person is bonded might be 500 to 1000 rupees...the slave must work for the slaveholders...[Debt] may carry into a second and third generation, growing under fraudulent accounting by the slaveholder."[41]

The problem of poverty is not limited to the developing world only. Between 1964 and 1996, as the pace of development and material progress boomed in America, poverty increased substantially. 13.8 percent of all Americans lived in poverty, 48 percent of whom were children.[42] One of the most extravagant cities in the world, New York witnessed an increase in the number of street-dwellers. This shows that being a signatory to the UN resolutions, international protocols and Humanitarian Laws is not adequate *per se*. Somehow, a sense of commitment to fight poverty has to be cultivated and this is immensely lacking in the developing and the developed world.

Chapter 5: Human Rights and Human Wrongs

Even without the biting recession that has pervaded the US economy, the equitable distribution of wealth, would have gone a long way in eradicating poverty in the most affluent nation in the world. The shouldering of responsibility by the rich nations could have alleviated poverty in the 'Third World', without causing havoc to the lives of millions.

One is flabbergasted to notice the increasing signs of poverty in the developed as well as oil-rich nations. Thirty years ago, one would have rarely come across people begging on the streets of London. But with an increase in homeless people sleeping on the pavements, people are forced into begging out of need.

In some oil-producing countries in the Middle East, one comes across distressing scenes of the disabled children begging for a small charity. This scene is becoming very common on the streets of Baghdad, where children torn apart by war are left with no other option but to beg. Sometimes, poor parents who would be living their daily life from hand to mouth might not have any other alternative. If the famous Ali Abbas, the child who lost both his legs and arms, together with all members of his family during the war, had not attracted the attention of the world media, he would not have been brought to Britain for treatment. What is conveniently forgotten is that there are hundreds of children who have been maimed because of war.

When one talks about poverty and victimization of civilians, the Western world cannot wash its hands of its direct responsibility and contribution in causing impoverishment of the Palestinian civilians, who had been dislodged from their homes.

The desolation and destitution that has befallen the Arab natives of Jerusalem can best be comprehended from the perspective of an observer in the field. Emma Williams presents an eye-witness account of her experiences, having lived in Jerusalem for two and a half years. She describes the life of constant fear and agony for the three million Palestinians. She writes: "The realities are ugly, difficult to talk about, difficult to believe: the brutality, the injustice, the silencing, the denial, the racism – above all, the Occupation." The wall is erected to divide Palestinian communities to make any settlement unworkable. In contrast with ghettos imposed on Jews in ancient Venice, or the apartheid system in South Africa, the segregation and restraints imposed on the occupied territories are much more severe. She writes that children are shot deliberately and the victims are always blamed. She cites the example of the shooting of the American student Rachel Corrie who was bulldozed by the Israelis. Illegal Jewish settlements thrive with all the modern amenities on the land snatched from the Palestinians, whereas, Palestinians are prohibited to build on their own land. "Daily the caged-in Palestinians watch the settlements bloom…" and pregnant women are witnessed dying at the Israeli checkpoints.[43]

Emma Williams quotes the Israeli newspaper *Ha'aretz's* report that "flechette shells (designed to explode into thousands of razor-sharp darts)" were fired at the children's football ground. The appeal to ban these shells was rejected by the Israeli court. She writes that Chris Hedges of the *New York Times* witnessed the Israeli soldiers provoking Palestinian children: "Come on dogs. Come! Son of a w----! Your mother's …" The *New York Times* reporter wrote: "…I have never before watched soldiers entice children like mice into a trap and murder them for sport". When the eye-witness reports happen to cross a barrage of censorship, 'freedom of expression' is further axed for the fear of being labelled as 'anti-Semitism'. The crux of the matter is that, "it doesn't get more racist than this: critics silenced because of the ethnicities involved…" Such is the state of the model democracy in the region which thrusts poverty on the people under occupation, on the basis of race. But there are many people of good conscience and humanitarian commitment in the West, who have the courage to expose the realities of human wrongs.

Children - The Silent Victims of Crimes against Humanity

INARTICULATE children, who are unaware of their human rights, are susceptible to all sorts of exploitation. In the United States, 15 million children live below the subsistence level; 22 percent below the age of 18 and 25 percent below the age of 12 live in hunger. In 1996, the daily birthrate of children in poverty was 2660 and the daily death-rate of children dying of hunger was 27. In 1995, 762,000 children lived in poverty in the city of New York. The number of homeless children was 10,000. It had doubled within seven years.[44] Children of poor families suffered abuse, including sub-standard education and violent deaths. The US ranks first among the rich countries of the world in child poverty.

The International Labour Organization Convention No. 182 (1999) has been ratified by 132 countries. It calls for "immediate action to ban the worst form of child labour".[45] 1.2 million children, boys and girls, are trafficked each year into abusive work, including the sex trade and armed conflicts.[46] According to Statistical Information and Monitoring Programme on Child Labour (SIMCO), there were 211 million children aged 5 - 14 in work in the year 2000.

The worst maltreatment of children has occurred in wars. In Africa, almost 120,000 children, aged 7 to 18 have been drawn into the armed conflicts.[47] In the next five to ten years, about 40 million children in Africa would have lost a parent because of the AIDS virus.[48] These children are vulnerable to be kidnapped and forced into fighting for the government forces or militias or rebels, and carry a very high risk of spreading AIDS. All these factors act as a time bomb in addition to the acute poverty from which the continent of Africa is suffering.

Chapter 6: Children – The Silent Victims of Crimes against Humanity

Major deliberations in the World Conference against Racism from 31 August – 7 September 2001 made appalling disclosures about worldwide human rights abuses of children. The conference focused on illegal trafficking of women and children, under a multi-billion dollar global industry, dominated by organized crime. Helpless victims are tricked, coerced and sold as slaves. In the United States alone, between 45,000 and 50,000 women and children are trafficked annually. Hundreds of thousands more are trafficked in Northern and Central Europe, Africa, Latin America and Asia.

The Conference paper under the title 'The Race Dimensions of Trafficking in Persons Especially Women and Children' identified a number of causes of unchecked abuse. It disclosed that during the Kosovo crisis, armed gangs abducted women and girls from refugee camps in Northern Albania to satisfy the carnal desires of wealthy foreign workers, including the United Nations peacekeepers, according to the paper. The traffickers use all sorts of inhuman and criminal methods to exploit women and under-aged girls. In order to keep them under their control, they use intimidation and involve them in never-ending debt bondage. But as the traffickers have high-profile connections, they are neither caught nor prosecuted.

Children of the women who had been raped are stigmatized and are subjected to discrimination at schools. The paper touched on the plight of these children who are deprived of opportunities to assimilate in society and live a normal life.

The paper under the title 'Racism against indigenous peoples' illustrated that the pre-Columbus population in North America of the native peoples was 10 to 12 million. By 1890, European settlers reduced it to about 300,000. It disclosed that in Australia, the children of Aborigines were forcibly separated from their parents and adopted by white families. Today these children are named 'Stolen Generation'. In the United States and Canada, the paper says, the native children were forbidden to speak their language. If they did, they were subjected to corporal punishment. Children were told that their parents had died, and parents were told that their children had died. This policy of lying was considered to be 'in the interest' of the American Indians. The Indians were prohibited from registering their births in order to deprive them of their civil rights. Racial discrimination still prevails against the children of the Indians in America, but this abuse is not given even a scant coverage in the media, perhaps in the interest of 'freedom of expression' and 'liberty'.

It was observed that there were 6,000 pending cases of child abuse against the Churches who ran residential schools on behalf of the Canadian government, and breached their position of trust. As a result of gross dishonesty, many of the victims of abuse and child molestation committed suicide. Should the outcome of the lawsuits turn out against these schools and residential homes, the Churches warn that they would almost certainly face bankruptcy. Whether this is a fair price for betrayal of trust, the church goers would have to decide for themselves.

The Conference paper under the title 'Working Far From Home – Migration and Discrimination', identified the refugee crisis. It said: "Women and children account for more than half of the refugees …96 per cent of children who work and sleep in the streets are migrants, half of them girls aged [between] 8 and 14".

The paper under the title 'All the Crossroads of Gender and Racial Discrimination' presented statistics of illiteracy. Out of the 960 million illiterate adults, two-thirds are women, and out of 1.3 billion people living in poverty, 70 per cent are women.

The most serious abuse in the present world, concerns children who do not even know what human rights are all about. Kevin Bales asserts: "In India…there are between 65 and 100 million children aged fourteen and younger who work more than eight hours a day."[49] About 15 million of these children are not child labourers but child slaves.[50] Due to the poverty and debt of their parents, they get trapped in the hands of greedy moneylenders and receive no wage for their labour.[51]

Bales makes shocking disclosures in his research on child slavery. It is estimated that there are 3000 household slaves in the major cities of the West, including Paris, London, New York, Zurich

Chapter 6: Children – The Silent Victims of Crimes against Humanity

and Los Angeles. He believes that the investment portfolios representing mutual and pension funds, own shares in corporations that employ bonded labour for the reason of minimizing cost and maximizing return.[52] Bales explains that, as opposed to the old slavery where the ownership of title used to pass through legally drawn-up documents, the new slavery is all about controlling the slaves. He cites a chilling account of an 11-year-old slave girl in an Amazonian gold mining town in Brazil. After she refused to entertain the lustful desires of a miner, he took his spiteful revenge by cutting her head off with a machete and then displaying it whilst other miners cheered and gave a gesture of support to him.[53]

In Africa, 90 percent of cocoa plantations in the Ivory Coast use slave labour of abducted children, as disclosed on BBC 24 *Reporters* documentary (27 May 2001). Several countries in South East Asia and Latin America too are involved in this menace. The furor in the British media over the shipment of the cargo of 200 child slaves in West Africa in April 2001 touched only a tip of the iceberg. Multinational companies struggle to procure their raw materials at cheap rates to maximize their profits, and this is done at the cost of victimizing children.

Cocoa is used in ice cream flavouring and in the manufacture of chocolates, enjoyed by millions in the West. But, as one slave labourer, who was never paid by the plantation owner, said: "It's like eating our flesh." The *Reporters* documentary focused on the acute problem of child slavery in cocoa farms in the Ivory Coast. Distressed parents believed that their children had been abducted to work on plantations. The programme highlighted the register in police possession, with names of children who had disappeared. Those who managed to escape the plantations provided ample evidence that the abuse does exist and yet, the chocolate-consuming countries shrug off their shoulders at the enormous human cost of luxury they enjoy.

Tourists who rejoice at getting bargain prices for the good-quality hand woven carpets from the sub-continent are equally oblivious. The tiny fingers of the 4 and 5-year-old children, work marvels for the profitability of the industry. The capital investment

Chapter 6: Children – The Silent Victims of Crimes against Humanity

of buying a child for forced labour is far less than procuring an automatic weaving machine. The operational cost of buying bread to feed a child is far cheaper than the expense of fuel needed to operate a machine.

Children in thousands are employed in the interior villages of India. The obvious hazard faced by them is the risk of getting their fingers cut off in the process of weaving carpets with bare hands. But then it is easy to replace disabled children simply because they are in abundant supply. Children need medical care against disease, illness and injury. Medicines cost money. These innocent children, with no one to comprehend their agony, pay the price of their parents' poverty and act as a cheap economic factor.

The owners of hazardous factories maintain their political links to make sure that their interest is protected under the watchful supervision of the influential politicians and corrupt police officers. This human calamity has been widely reported by field researchers in India and yet the offenders walk free. Their friends in the important government positions make sure that even if they are caught, they are released without any charge.

In India, the Juvenile Justice Act of 1986 does not cover children under the age of 14 because they are not supposed to be working. Hence, the legislature has chosen to turn a blind eye towards the burning issue of the day that is robbing the children of their fundamental human rights. Children suffer from brutal treatment, torture and rape. The bureaucratic and indifferent attitude of the Juvenile Welfare Board has been a contributory factor in failing to bring the offending employers to justice, as reported in the Indian press.

In North Bihar 4,000 - 5,000 children are kidnapped every year and forced into slavery to make carpets. They are beaten by the slave masters to make them work at midnight and in the early hours of the morning. In India's carpet factories, as many as 300,000 children remain slaves. They put up with horrendous living conditions. They are allowed to go up on the roof of the factories to answer the call of nature. They are not allowed to leave the four walls of their work 'prison'.

Chapter 6: Children – The Silent Victims of Crimes against Humanity

Children work in various industries, such as carpet weaving, cloth printing, dyeing, tanning, explosives, fireworks, match manufacturing, mines, chemicals, pesticides, and other harmful industries. Children are also committed into immoral professions. Almost 80 percent of India's child workers are engaged on farms as bonded labour, working to pay their parents' debts to the covetous moneylenders. A growing number of abducted children, with a leg or arm amputated, also work for the Mafia that controls street begging. In Egypt, the Mafia of beggars controls begging in the close proximity of mosques and cinemas, where the chances of earning charity money are bright.

A feudal system under the 'high caste' thugs, very much exists in India. It exploits the poor and simple-minded 'low caste' people. A combination of complicated customs and superstitions are used to control the honour and dignity of 'inferior' human beings. Interest rates on loans given to the peasants by the landlords in inner villages of India can go as high as 60 percent.[54]

Juddith Ennew, in her well-illustrated book[55] presents the painful plight of bonded children who work as home servants, shoe-polishers, rag-pickers, carpet weavers, rubbish collectors, agricultural workers, brick carriers and so forth. Case studies have been cited of children exposed to dangerous chemicals without any protection. Ranging from parental poverty to abduction, children in countries, such as the Philippines, Thailand, Vietnam, India, Nepal, and Sri Lanka, are forced into selling their bodies to rich tourists from the United States and Europe. Children are given addictive drugs so that they may not demand payment. The most terrifying plight of children in Thailand has been presented in several TV documentaries. Poverty-stricken parents are forced to sell their children, who are taken away by the buyers straight into the sex industry. The immoral industry thrives because of the paedophile tourists from the United States and Europe.

Judith Ennew demonstrates the rough conditions in which children live on streets, farms and factories. In 1989, the United Nations adopted the Convention on the Rights of the Child. In 1992, the South Asian Coalition of Child Servitude (SACCS) freed

Chapter 6: Children – The Silent Victims of Crimes against Humanity

children from slavery in northern India's carpet industry. In recent years, children in developing countries have made their voices heard by petitioning directly to the governments and heads of States. The pressure group 'United Children' has been formed to fight for the rights of child workers.

Pakistan passed the Bonded Labour Abolition Act in 1992. The Human Rights commission of Pakistan estimates that there are in the region of 20 million forced labour workers in the country. Pakistan has child labour of over nine million. Employers prefer to substitute adults with child labour by paying them less wages, with no fear of bargaining. As the carpet industry is labour-intensive, it employs the largest number of child workers.

Poverty, illiteracy and social conditions are the main causes, as well as the major obstacles for taking any action against child exploitation. Children leave school at a very early age, with the risk of ending up on streets and becoming victims of manipulation by the slave-masters. Some grow up to become mentally disturbed and resort to drug addiction and violence.

Jonathan Silvers reckons there are half a million to one million children between four and fourteen working full-time in carpet weaving in Pakistan. UNICEF believes that they make up 90 percent of the carpet industry's workforce. "Much of the nation's farmland is worked by ...yoked teams of three-, four-, and five-year-olds who plough, seed and glean fields from dawn to dusk" the author writes. A painful account of a mother called Asma is told. She taught her children that for the survival of the family, they are expected to make sacrifices. When the time came, her children willingly took bondage to live with strangers from the age of five. The slave-masters often abuse their strength and beat the children. The punishments to which children are subjected include hanging them upside down, starvation and caning. Some factory owners also employ armed gangs to attack investigatory teams. The police side with the factory owners. The Bonded Labour Liberation Front has succeeded in liberating thousands of children from bonded labour and thousands of high court cases were won against unscrupulous industrialists and feudalists. Half of Pakistan's child workers die by the age of twenty because of the unhealthy working environment.[56]

There was also the much-publicized tragic plight of the 4- and-5-year-old Pakistani and Bangladeshi children who had been abducted and smuggled out of their countries by boat to the United Arab Emirates, to help entertain in the camel races. These tiny children were trained to become jockeys at enormous risk to their lives. Channel 4 televised a programme, *Innocent Slot* (8 and 9 December 1997) on the exploitation of children under various cultures. The most moving part was the inhuman treatment to which children who were bought in bondage from hospitals in Bangladesh were subjected. When they were placed on the backs of camels, they cried and screamed with fear, which made the camels run faster. As the price money was irresistibly attractive, winning the camel race was crucial for the camel owners. Children testified in the documentary that they were starved to keep them light and slim. They said that they had fallen many times from the backs of the camels.

At global level, the International Programme for the Elimination of Child Labour has been initiated. There is a growing awareness among the humanitarian agencies that changing the catastrophic circumstance of millions of juveniles around the world must not be left to the whims of individual countries. It is not sufficient to make occasional noises in the media about child abuse. It is through the untiring efforts of the non-governmental human rights activists that concrete solutions would be forthcoming.

Amidst an international outrage during the last thirteen years, the children of Iraq suffered from an acute shortage of food and basic medical care. Robin Cook, who resigned his cabinet post as Leader of the House of Commons over the Iraq war was a supporter of sanctions. It is worth recalling what he had to say to the House of Commons in his capacity as Secretary of State for Foreign and Commonwealth Affairs. The Human Rights Report that he presented in July 2000 justified the sanctions against Iraq despite the fact that the suffering of the Iraqi people had "attracted widespread condemnation", as he himself put it. He told the House that the British Government rejected the argument that sanctions were

Chapter 6: Children – The Silent Victims of Crimes against Humanity

responsible. Revenues from illegal oil sales were being wasted on new palaces and theme parks. He said that Saddam celebrated his birthday with a cake three meters high whose ingredients would have fed 100 children for 30 days. Instead of buying much-needed food and medicine with this revenue, the report said, Saddam spent it on "10,000 bottles of whisky and 50 million cigarettes each month." (p. 18).

Some distinction had to be drawn between the ethical responsibility of the democratic nations who were behind the sanctions, and the savage totalitarian regime of Saddam, who did not give a toss about the interests of the Iraqi people. The children of Iraq were caught up in this terrible obstinacy. The magnitude of the problem should not have been trivialized with rhetoric, as innocent lives were being lost every hour during the enforcement of unjustified sanctions. The lives of not one hundred, but several millions of children deprived of food and medicine, through no fault of their own, were at risk. Nobody asked for the approval of the children of Iraq before building palaces and theme parks. So why were they being punished?

Perhaps the worst part of crime against children is when they are caught up in a vicious cycle of violence. In May 1990, the year in which the UN World Summit on Children was held in New York, a 1000-page situation report was presented by the Swedish Save the Children Organization. It reported that, "the Israeli army had systematically become child-killers". The report said that between December 1987 and December 1989, "159 children under age 16 were killed by soldiers. The average age of dead was 10. Between 50,000 and 63,000 children were beaten, gassed or wounded". But less than a month after the publication of that report, George Bush Senior used his veto power, according to the report, to "block a Security Council Resolution calling for sending UN observers to investigate Israeli violations of Palestinian human rights."[57] What can be said about this veto? Was the core human rights issue being decided on the basis of race and ethnicity?

The Save the Children Organization had filed its report on the systematic killings of Palestinian children during the first

Chapter 6: Children – The Silent Victims of Crimes against Humanity

intifada (uprising). After the outbreak of the second *intifada*, the occupying force broke all the records of human scruples by using live ammunitions, with shoot-to-kill orders against the stone-throwing Arab children – the measures it would never ever conceive of taking against Jewish children.

Michael Palumbo in his impressive book *Imperial Israel* calls the first *intifada* as 'children's crusade' because most of the casualties were children. He gives some of the most shocking and chilling accounts of how "force, power and blows" were used by Yitzhak Rabin, the then Defence Minister in 1988 to quell the *intifada*. He gives eye-witness accounts of incidents that took place right in front of Karen White, an American journalist. A boy of nine or ten was pulled by his hair, dragged and kicked in his face and chest. A group of Israeli soldiers laughed "as they kicked a feeble old man in the genitals..." writes Palumbo.[58]

Human rights abuses were observed by foreign correspondents in hospitals, confirmed by Amnesty International Report, where Israeli soldiers entered operating theatres and dragged out the wounded.[59] The teeth of an 8-year-old boy were broken because "the soldiers thought he wanted to throw a stone".[60]

In the aftermath of the first *intifada* in December 1987, the whole education system was sealed, including schools and universities. Institutes of Higher Education were closed down for over four years. David McDowall writes: "Kindergarten children are not usually classed as agents of sedition, but that is how Israel treated them. Schools remained closed for two consecutive years."[61] Through its action, Israel in effect prepared the cadre for the second *intifada*.

Local communities seeking to continue educating their young ones at home, or at mosque or church were threatened in August 1988 that they would be locked up for ten years. When schools reopened in 1990, many children had dropped out.[62] Thus, Israel sought to ruin an entire generation of Palestinians – something it would never have wished for the children of Jewish immigrants, who had lived under Nazi persecution.

The CNN presented reports from the occupied territories and

Chapter 6: Children – The Silent Victims of Crimes against Humanity

from inside Israel on 6 and 7 August 2001, regarding the psychosomatic suffering of civilians as a result of continuous violence. Children in the occupied territories have been suffering from a state of shock and emotional trauma, which will take more than international aid to heal. As a consequence of indiscriminate shelling and demolition of houses, young people and children have been left with physical and mental scars. The future of these children was being systematically destroyed whilst the world watched the horrifying crime against humanity. The United Nations did not feel morally obliged to intervene under the circumstances by sending UN troops into the area because of the US dictates.

The developed world is a co-partner in the abuse of children's rights. In Britain, the latest scandal of the asylum policy has witnessed youngsters, including babies being held in detention centres. Asylum-seeker juveniles of 13–17 years of age live in bed-and-breakfast or bed-sit accommodation. *The Independent* writes: "In 2002, 5945 children aged 17 and under sought asylum…", with 6000 refugee children under social services care.[63]

At governmental and private levels, violations of children's human rights have crossed all the civilized standards and values.

7

Instruments of Crime - Lethal Weapons, Small Arms and Nuclear Proliferation

THE civil war in the Democratic Republic of Congo has claimed the life of three million people in the last five years. There is no scarcity of arms for the warring parties. The country, formerly known as Zaire, was controlled by the dictator Mobutu. The United States and Israel enjoyed cherished relations with him for several decades and supplied him with experts and consultants. The country was the producer of diamonds, which were smuggled out to finance the country's self-liquidating war.

Similarly, foreign powers have an inherent interest in the civil wars in Sierra Leone and the Ivory Coast. Children are exploited, armed and forced into the conflicts. As far as the warlords are concerned, the bloodbath is merely an investment for them. If they and their party could make it to the top, then in six months they could recover their investment with colossal gain.

In the Cold War era, many developing nations had suffered human rights abuses under the influence of Communism. Ethiopia had endured acute starvation for many years under its dictatorial rulers. The suffering of the people continues up to this day as a chain of sequence. The Ethiopian government exported grain and agricultural produce that were badly needed by the starving public, to the former Soviet Union in exchange for arms. The military junta's priority was to finance military spending of the largest army in Sub-Saharan Africa. The arms were needed by the despots not to fight an external enemy, but to enslave their own people. Once they grabbed power and started to reap the benefit of the wealth of their nation, they were not prepared to relinquish it voluntarily.

Chapter 7: Instruments of Crime – Lethal Weapons, Small Arms and Nuclear Proliferation

As their grip on power tightens, the unrepresentative governments tend to stockpile various types of weapons and ammunition which they are not even capable of using. Therefore, under the arms contracts, they are bound to employ experts from abroad at immense salaries to train their armies in the use of new weaponry.

For a long time, the need to control the menace of arms proliferation was felt at international level. The first UN Conference on the Illicit Trade in Small Arms and Light Weapons in All its Aspects was held in New York in July 2001. The Protocol against the Illicit Manufacturing of and Trafficking in Firearms, their Parts, Components and Ammunition was adopted by the UN General Assembly on 31 May 2001.

The Human Rights Report 2001 of the Foreign and Commonwealth Office in London identifies four measures that the British government has adopted for controlling the proliferation of small arms and light weapons: (i) to cut back light weapons falling into the wrong hands, (ii) to conduct a worldwide campaign on 'conflict diamonds and illegal drugs', (iii) to issue guidelines on the ways of responding to humanitarian crises, and (iv) to assist UN peacekeeping operations. (p. 59).

Control over Lethal Weapons

On 25 July 2001, the United States rejected an agreement to ban the use of biological weapons under the pretext that it would expose American businesses to industrial espionage. The countries that signed the UN Convention were expected to succumb to the interests of American corporations. The American representative alleged that the protocol would put his country's security at risk. This means that the entry of international inspectors onto the sites producing biological weapons in the United States was out of the question. But other countries were expected to welcome the inspectors into their facilities.

On the control of Biological Weapons, 144 States ratified the

Chapter 7: Instruments of Crime – Lethal Weapons, Small Arms and Nuclear Proliferation

1972 Convention on the Prohibition of the Development, Stockpiling, and Use of Bacteriological (Biological) and Toxin Weapons and on their Destruction (Biological Weapons Convention).

Human Rights Watch World Report 2001 states that 140 States ratified the 1993 Convention on the Prohibition of the Development, Production, Stockpiling, and Use of Chemical Weapons and on their Destruction (Chemical Weapons Convention). The body overseeing the implementation of the Convention is the Organization for the Prohibition of Chemical Weapons (OPCW).

There was an extensive use of Landmines in the conflicts in Kosovo and Chechnya. Between November 1999 and October 2000, 107 nations ratified the 1997 Convention on the Prohibition of the Use, Stockpiling, Production and Transfer of Antipersonnel Mines and On Their Destruction (Mine Ban Treaty).

In May 1998, the Clinton Administration declared that the United States would join the Mine Ban Treaty in 2006, if the Pentagon succeeded by that time to identify the alternatives. For a second year in a row in 2000, the Pentagon asked for $48 million for a new mine system called RADAM that would contain, not only antitank mines, but also antipersonnel mines, banned under the Mine Ban Treaty. Human Rights Watch also discovered that the US Air Force planned to stockpile antipersonnel mines in Qatar, which itself was a party to the Mine Ban Treaty.

The International Atomic Energy Agency reported on 13 August 2001 that people living in more than 70 countries, mostly in the developing world, face the 'silent menace' daily. An estimated 60 million buried and abandoned landmines still exist. About 26,000 people are killed and many more are disabled every year, due to undiffused landmines. It is mostly women, children and farmers, who are the victims of the uncleared and buried explosives.

The report says: "At a time when societies need to learn to live and work together, mines have the triple effect of shattering individual lives, increasing the medical burden...and preventing states from developing land and rebuilding infrastructures."[64]

Several UN agencies address this issue. The UN Children's Fund (UNICEF) provides guidance for mine awareness programmes. The UN office for the Co-ordination of Humanitarian Affairs (OCHA) shares information on the implications of landmines. The World Health Organization (WHO) and the World Food Programme (WFP) also provide useful services for assisting the victims. The United Nations Development Programme (UNDP) assists in developing national mine clearance capacities.

The users of anti-personnel mines are able to inflict casualties on innocent civilians, especially children, long after the conflicts are over. The UN General Assembly passed Resolution 51/45S on 10 December 1996, urging all states to pursue vigorously an effective and legally binding international agreement to ban the use, stockpiling, production and transfer of anti-personnel landmines. Non-governmental agencies also play an effective role in alleviating suffering and in campaigning that a distinction must be drawn between the combatants and civilians.

The Convention on the Prohibition of the Use, Stockpiling, Production and Transfer of Anti-Personnel Mines and on their Destruction was passed at Oslo, Norway on 18 September 1997. It consists of 22 Articles, with detailed procedural guidance to the state parties. Since December 1997, when opened for signatures, 140 states joined. Out of these, 117 members gave their consent to be bound by the provisions of Mine Ban Treaty.

The International Campaign to Ban Landmines (ICBL) called on the G8 leaders meeting in Genoa to step up action against mines. It urged Russia and the United States, the only members of the G8 who remain outside the treaty, to reaffirm their commitment to join the Mine Ban Treaty.[65] The ICBL won the 1997 Nobel Peace Prize for its endeavours to secure the 1997 Mine Ban Treaty.

Chapter 7: Instruments of Crime – Lethal Weapons, Small Arms and Nuclear Proliferation

Control over Small Arms

Arms sales are closely connected with violations of human rights. It would be naïve to imagine otherwise. The Parliamentary Assembly of the Council of Europe, in a resolution adopted on 27 September 1989 (resolution 928) declared that, "...purchase of arms often were pursued at the expense of the economic and social development of countries in the so-called 'Third World' countries." It also stated that many arms exports may be used for violations of human rights over which the exporting country has no control, except what it called, to "refuse to export arms which could be used for domestic repression."

Paragraph (g) of the resolution speaks of the necessity of urging the 'Third World' countries to allocate their scarce resources to "civilian investment, rather than excessive armament". It recommends that this factor be taken into account when approving development aid and relief from debt. It urges the necessity of promoting democracy and human rights in these countries.[66]

Small arms include revolvers and self-loading pistols, rifles, sub-machine guns, assault rifles and light machine-guns. Light weapons include heavy machine-guns, some types of grenade launchers, portable anti-aircraft and anti-tank guns, and portable launchers of anti-aircraft missile systems. Ammunition and explosives are construed as part of small arms and light weapons.

According to the United Nations, four million people, many of them women and children have been killed with light arms in the last ten years, which means, at the rate of 1095 per day. Therefore, the need for controlling their proliferation and limiting their accessibility is self-explanatory.

The UN Conference on the Illicit Trade in Small Arms and Light Weapons recognized from the outset that there are 100 odd countries that need these arms for legitimate self-defence. But how can one draw a line of demarcation between the security and self-defence needs of the States and that of the high-handed policies of the States?

Chapter 7: Instruments of Crime – Lethal Weapons, Small Arms and Nuclear Proliferation

Robin Cook, the ex-Foreign and Commonwealth Secretary of the United Kingdom rightly noted in his address, the transcript of which dated 24 September 1999, was included in the papers at the Conference. He said: "...[W]e really need a different phrase than 'small arms'. There has been nothing 'small' about the misery they have brought to families or the disruption they have brought to societies. ...Most of the conflicts have taken place in the developing world, but most of the firearms were made in the industrialized world".

Then Robin Cook observed that there might be as many as 500 million weapons in circulation, more than personal computers in the world. He said that the European Union has agreed a joint action of restraint from equipping groups outside legitimate governments.

Among the papers at the Conference was the transcript dated 24 September 1999 of the speech of Mrs Madeleine Albright, the ex-Secretary of State of the United States. The transcript read, "United Nations of America" and not "United States of America". Ironically, many sceptics in the 'Third World' do believe that the United Nations is of America.

She stressed: "Countries that are among the world's poorest spend hundreds of millions of dollars buying small arms and other weapons. Funds are diverted, crops are mortgaged and relief supplies are stolen to finance these purchases." This would have been the most appropriate time to announce concrete measures that the US would be prepared to take to ban such weapons altogether from the poor countries. But words were not translated into action.

Working Papers by the President of the Conference, consisting of 21 clauses, recognized the devastating consequences on children and displacement of civilians, due to proliferation of small arms. This necessitated urgent action and co-operation at global, regional, sub-regional, and national levels to combat, control or reduce the supply and demand of these weapons.

Though the Conference covered many aspects of controlling the proliferation of lethal and small arms, the Working Papers recognized that these arms would be needed by States to assert their right of self-determination. Therefore, Clause 10 states: "Reaffirming also the right of self-determination of all peoples, in particular under colonial or other forms of alien domination or foreign occupation, and the importance of the effective realization of this right ..."

Hence, there was a clear provision in the Working Papers of the Conference and explicit recognition at global level that the inalienable right of indigenous people fighting for self-determination from foreign occupation is to be upheld.

In order to keep its own small arms industry buoyant, the United States did not give its consent to the agreement reached in a two-week Conference to curb the small arms trade. David Usborne writes: "...Washington's tactics was felt most strongly among African governments..."[67]

In the past, Ronald Brown the former US Secretary of Commerce for Arms had pronounced vividly the US policy on arms supplies. He said that the only recognized 'moral imperative' of the US is not to restrain the export of arms but to protect the jobs and security of the American people, so that the US can enjoy the status of 'most powerful nation in the world'.

Control over Nuclear Proliferation

On 1 August 1949, The United States Atomic Energy Commission submitted a report to the Congress stressing the positive aspects of the development of atomic energy. It took ten years to negotiate a Treaty for Non-Proliferation of Nuclear Weapons. At last, the Treaty was signed on 1 July 1968. Three nuclear powers, the UK, the US and the former Soviet Union added their signatures. China, the fourth nuclear power, was not a member of the United Nations, so it was not invited to sign. France, the fifth nuclear power abstained from voting and eight weeks later, it exploded a hydrogen bomb in the South Pacific.[68]

Since 1945 more than 1032 nuclear tests are attributable to the US alone, out of the total blasts of 2000. Many more sub-critical

Chapter 7: Instruments of Crime – Lethal Weapons, Small Arms and Nuclear Proliferation

tests were also carried out. The Non-Proliferation Treaty (NPT), Partial Test Ban Treaty (PTBT) and Comprehensive Test Ban Treaty (CTBT) plus the imposition of sanctions were meant to ensure that the nuclear proliferation did not go out of the absolute control of the gang of five. China was accepted as a member of the club only reluctantly, out of fear and not out of choice. The author of the Paper on CTBT stresses: "Had China been of the same white racial stock, one wonders if the hullabaloo on CTBT or NPT would have been of the same magnitude..."[69]

On 12 April 1995, 50 states ratified the Convention on Nuclear Safety. Out of these, 45 states with the notable exception of India and Israel, attended the First Review Meeting in Vienna from 12-23 April 1999 at the headquarters of the International Atomic Energy Agency (IAEA). The aim of the Convention was to achieve a high level of nuclear safety worldwide. Membership in the Convention incorporates exchange of information, and answers questions posed by the Contracting Parties on safety measures.

The participants were coordinating with each other in good faith in the global interest. They did not have anything to fear and did not have any secretive motives. The Contracting Parties took vital measures to establish independent self-regulatory bodies and streamline the management procedures in the interest of bilateral and multilateral co-operation. Matters of international concern addressed by the Contracting Parties included the prevailing safety measures in the case of serious accidents, and the shutting down of the nuclear installations, if need be. Changes in technological development affecting nuclear power plants, the obsolescence of equipment in use, and the engagement of outside expertise to update and upgrade the facilities were considered of paramount importance.

A Quality Assurance programme based on best international practices was the ultimate goal. Exchange of data on the Radiation Protection System required an open-door policy at international level, with the need to review and evaluate the lessons learnt.

The purpose of the Treaty signed by the States Parties was to devise principles and objectives for nuclear non-proliferation, nuclear disarmament and international co-operation in the peaceful uses of nuclear energy, with the ultimate aim of eliminating completely nuclear weapons. The signatories to the Treaty recognized the need for the creation of nuclear-weapons-free-zones for global and regional peace and security.

Resolution 984 (1995) was passed by the UN Security Council unanimously, concerning the security assurances and internationally legally binding commitments. Transparency in nuclear-related exports and the completion of the negotiations in connection with the Nuclear Test Ban Treaty are emphasized in the resolution.

The General Assembly adopted Resolution 49/71 on 15 December 1994 by consensus, for the establishment of a nuclear-weapons-free-zone in the Middle East. Clause 4 of the Resolution on the Middle East is very important in view of the unstable situation in the region. It is interesting to note that the Resolution reaffirms 'the universal adherence to the Treaty', and calls upon all states of the Middle East that have not yet done so, 'without exception', to accept the Treaty without delay and to place their nuclear facilities 'under full scope of International Atomic Energy Agency safeguards'.

In spite of the emphatic recommendation by the United Nations, Israel with the support of the US has simply rebuffed the resolution. It has not signed the Treaty on the Non-Proliferation of Nuclear Weapons. Lack of will and determination on the part of the UN to enforce international accords and agreements for the control of biological, chemical and nuclear weapons is being disregarded by the parties who are not the signatories.

In a detailed discourse on Pakistan's nuclear capabilities, the author of the paper 'Dual Deterrence – Pakistan's Strategic Bonus' (1998)[70] describes the dual role the US played in relation to the nuclear status of India and Pakistan. In retrospect, it seemed that the US considered Pakistan its ally. But when the scare of the so-called 'Islamic Bomb' was blown out of proportion, sanctions were imposed through international financing agencies. At no time were the 200 nuclear warheads of Israel considered a threat to world peace. The US viewed India as a strategic partner in economic development and a 'global nuclear actor', to use the words of Henry Kissinger.

Nuclear bombs in the hands of the big nations are as dangerous, detestable and undesirable as they are in the hands of small states. History proves that whenever this bomb was used, it brought nothing but cataclysm.

The previous US governments are known to have written off billions of dollars of debts to Israel, in addition to several billions that are remitted as tax-free aid every year. This does not include the military assistance that Israel gets in money and in kind under joint military ventures between the two countries.

The Middle East is an ultra-sensitive region because it has always been susceptible to the political rivalries of other nations. Its rich resources and oil make it vulnerable to proxy wars and disputes. For the safety of the people in the region, the Middle East should be made totally free from nuclear weapons. After Chernobyl, vigilance is the best policy. After Chernobyl, no safety measures can be trusted.

The case history of Chernobyl leaves many lessons to be learnt by the world community. Prior to the nuclear accident in Ukraine in 1986, the former Soviet Union had taken all the possible precautions. Yet, the explosions at the Chernobyl nuclear reactors did happen, leaving health hazards that would affect life in Ukraine for at least seventy years.

Helicopters were used round the clock to extinguish the fire by dropping, as Gilbert writes, "five thousand tons of lead, limestone, sand and boron". The disaster to human life was atrocious. Apart from 250 deaths, hundreds of thousands of people had to be evacuated as there was high radioactive material in the air.[71]

The Soviet leaders adopted a conspiracy of silence for three days. Some twenty countries, including Britain were affected with the passing poisonous clouds. Scientists predicted high risk in cancer-related deaths, with adverse effect on livestock.[72] The

Chapter 7: Instruments of Crime – Lethal Weapons, Small Arms and Nuclear Proliferation

damage was to extend well into the twenty-first century.

The government of Ukraine announced in 1992 that between 6,000 and 8,000 people had been killed by the nuclear disaster.[73] In the investigatory report of the European Union in 1996, scientists from eight different countries reached the shocking conclusion that out of the total population of just over fifty million, thirty million Ukrainians might be at risk from contamination of radioactive material.[74]

In a conference held jointly between the United Nations Atomic Energy Agency and European Commission in April 1996, a Soviet expert made a stunning disclosure. He said, "radioactivity from the Chernobyl accident was two hundred times greater than that from the Hiroshima and Nagasaki atom bombs combined".[75] The main victims of the disaster, as in the past, are children with high deformed births and infant mortality rate.

The nuclear powers themselves should set an example in the interest of the world peace to start destroying their nuclear arsenal. But the blatant hypocrisy has not stopped short of even using the International Atomic Energy Agency to enforce double standards. The nations that have not signed the non-proliferation treaty are free to develop and spread the menace as they like and to bully their neighbours. There is a cause of alarm only if they are not in the US camp of influence. If the IAEA is to preserve its credibility, then it has to act impartially, outside the influence of the world powers.

8

Torture and War Crimes

THE Universal Declaration of Human Rights declares: "All human beings are born free and equal in dignity and rights. They are endowed with reason and conscience and should act towards one another in a spirit of brotherhood." (Clause A1) "No one shall be subjected to torture or to cruel, inhuman or degrading treatment or punishment." (Clause A5) "No one shall be subjected to arbitrary arrest, detention or exile." (Clause A9)

The modern Human Rights movement sprang from the dismay felt by many people that any government had the audacity of abusing, imprisoning, torturing, and killing human beings just because they have different beliefs from their governments.[76]

The UN Convention on Civil and Political Rights forbids torture and inhuman or degrading treatment, slavery or involuntary servitude, arbitrary arrest and detention, and 'debtor's prisons'. It forbids propaganda advocating either war or hatred based on race, religion, national origin, or language. After almost two decades of negotiations and rewriting, the text of the Universal Covenant on Civil and Political Rights was agreed upon in 1966. In 1976, after being ratified by the required 35 states, it became international law, according to United Nations Agreements on Human Rights.

The UN Convention Against Torture bans torture under all circumstances. It requires states to take effective legal and other measures to prevent torture. It declares that no state of emergency, other external threats or orders from a superior officer or authority may be invoked to justify torture. The Convention was passed in February 1985.

Article 1 of the Convention elaborates that "…torture means any act by which severe pain or suffering, whether physical or mental, is intentionally inflicted on a person for such purposes as obtaining from him or a third person information or a confession...." Public officials or anybody acting on their behalf are bound by the Convention.

Article 2 states that the State Party shall take effective legislative, administrative, judicial or other measures to prevent acts of torture. This is a common clause found in almost all the UN Declarations, recommending to the signatories that their domestic law should be compliant with international law. It also states that no recourse is available to any exceptional circumstances to justify torture.

Article 4 specifies that not only torture but an attempt to commit torture is an offence under criminal law and Article 5 provides guidance to State Parties as to the measures they ought to take under their jurisdiction over the offences committed.

Procedures for the appointment of a Committee against Torture, and the rights of the State Parties in the election by secret ballot and rules for convening the meetings are elaborated. The investigation and reporting procedure of the elected Committee, its liaison and its terms of reference vis-à-vis the State Parties are covered at length. The rules of arbitration for settling disputes between State Parties and the International Court of Justice are stated in detail.

The right of the Parties to denounce the Convention is also protected, but it is clarified, that this in itself will not absolve their obligation from abiding by the Convention prior to denunciation.

When the Convention against Torture was opened for signatures at the United Nations Headquarters in New York on 4 February 1985, the United States, Israel and Yugoslavia were not among the signatories.

In the first international Conference of Amnesty International on the Abolition of Torture, held in Paris in December 1973, its Chairman said in his opening speech: "...There is no doubt it [torture] is practised with the direct or implied permission of a large number of governments, many of whom consider themselves civilized. ...Like a contagious disease, it spreads from one country to another..."[77] In the ongoing conflicts, it is practised on political

Chapter 8 : Torture and War Crimes

prisoners. Though the world is told that torture is illegal under the domestic laws, no impartial observers are allowed in the prisons to verify for themselves.

The 2001 Report of Amnesty International on human rights violations covers 149 countries. The report blames, what it calls, "excessive use of lethal force by Israeli security services" which caused the deaths of hundreds of Palestinians, including children. The report also recognizes that Lebanese prisoners were held in the Khiam detention centre for over 15 years without charge during Israel's occupation of South Lebanon. This literally means that Israel held them hostages to be used as 'bargaining chips'.

On the abhorrent conditions in the Concentration Camp of Khiam, Amnesty reports: "Prior to the Israeli withdrawal, Lebanese nationals continued to be detained outside any legal framework in Khiam...where conditions were cruel, inhuman and degrading and torture was systematic." Yet, the people who succeeded in freeing themselves from the sadistic brutality of occupation were categorized as 'terrorists'.

Under the illegal and immoral occupation of South Lebanon for 22 years, Lebanese nationals were arrested, tortured and detained without trial. Their family members were kidnapped and used as human shields. But when the two Israeli soldiers were abducted, Israel capitalized on the incident to create a dispute with the United Nations, alleging that the UN observers had failed in their duty. Hence, the Israeli government used this incident in support of its outright rejection to allow UN observers in the occupied territories.

Amnesty's delegates found that Israeli forces had used, in their words, "high explosive weapons, such as the M203 grenade launcher in residential area". The report also makes references to 'extra-judicial executions' and the 'policy of liquidations'. It observes: "Unlawful killings of Palestinians continued and Israel's policy of closures has cut off Palestinian towns and villages ..." Such an inexorable state of affairs has continued without paying any heed to international opinion or humanitarian standards.

During the years of the first *Intifada*, 100,000 Palestinians were detained. The Public Committee Against Torture in Israel was founded by a prominent group of academics, human rights attorneys, human rights activists and professionals. In 1996 the Organization was the recipient of the Human Rights Award of the French Republic. The group reports that the torture of Palestinians has continued ever since the occupation of the West Bank and Gaza despite the fact that in 1991, Israel ratified the United Nations Convention Against Torture and Other Cruel, Inhuman or Degrading Treatment or Punishment.

The Public Committee Against Torture in Israel, based in Jerusalem, describes the plight of the Palestinians in the course of interrogation by the Israeli forces. In its report it identifies various methods involved, which include, "...verbal and psychological abuse, threats against the individual or the individual's family, lack of adequate clothing or hygiene, food and sleep deprivation, tying up the detainee on a little chair in painful positions for hours or days on end, covering of the head with a wet and/or stinking sack, blasting of unbearably loud music..." Other repressive measures include imprisonment in small cubicles and holding the detainees in confinement by refusing them any contact with a legal representative. Torture also extended, according to the report, to "exposure to cold through outside elements or the blasting of air conditioners, forced physical exercise for excruciating periods, beatings, violent shaking of the head and the body..." The report states that Palestinians are rounded up daily and the torture leaves physical and mental damage on the detainees who are held without charge.[78]

Amnesty International's Report 2001 also gives a harrowing account of electric shocks, beatings, and torture as a means of state policy. One detainee said that Israeli officers "stuffed his mouth with stones, poured water over his face, kicked him in the genitals and smashed his head...."

Michael Palumbo's book *Imperial Israel* provides a thorough background to the history of occupation of the West Bank and Gaza. He outlines the factors that triggered *intifada* in the occupied territories in December 1987. Since 1967, Palestinians in the West Bank and Gaza had to undergo, in his words, "...relentless beatings,

Chapter 8 : Torture and War Crimes

torture, deportations, shooting, seizure of land, closing of schools and every other conceivable form of abuse".[79]

The Sunday Times of London as long back as thirty years ago published an extensive report on widespread use of torture in Israeli prisons and detention centres. It concluded that, "torture of Arab prisoners is so widespread and systematic that it cannot be dismissed as 'rogue cops' exceeding orders. It [torture] appears to be sanctioned as deliberate policy."[80] James A. Joyce wrote that *The Sunday Times* "broke through the silence barrier with which the press of Britain and America has muffled the ugly practices going on in the occupied territories ever since Israel quadrupled its geographical size in 1967 by invading its four Arab neighbours...."[81]

The Sunday Times changed the trend followed by most papers in those days of blaming the UN Human Rights Commission for attacking Israel and not doing anything about torture practised by Idi Amin in Uganda. The deformed rationale was that because Idi Amin adopted vile practices, so torture practised by Israel had to be tolerated, otherwise this would be a discrimination against Israel or 'anti-Semitism'. The UN investigating teams were denied any access in the occupied territories in those days, in as much as they were denied access in Jenin in the aftermath of the dreadful massacre in 2002.

The Israeli embassy in London responded to *The Sunday Times* article, saying that if evidence is presented, then the government would make, "every effort to investigate". Joyce reminds that the fact which is continuously and deliberately ignored is that "occupation itself is illegal *ab initio* and a flagrant denial of the principles of the UN Charter and the Universal Declaration of Human Rights, as well as of international law in general". She continues that the "Israelis cannot be right, whatever arguments they employ, so long as their occupation of Arab lands continues to affront civilized mankind...."[82]

Israeli inhuman measures left no other alternative for the Palestinians than the *intifada* in the 1980s and the second *intifada* since September 2000. Several stories of the prisoners who were subjected to ugly methods of torture have been told. A detailed

Chapter 8 : Torture and War Crimes

account is also given of the subhuman state in which prisoners were detained in the Negev desert. [83]

During the *intifada* in the 1980s Jewish settlers mutilated the bodies of the Palestinians whom they murdered, and even burnt some alive. Joyce writes: "It is tragically ironic, in view of the Holocaust, that the Israelis should use poison gas against civilians. And it is disturbing that the gas canisters are clearly marked 'Made in Salzburg, Pennsylvania, USA'. "[84]

The UN General Assembly passed Resolution 2433 [XXIII] on 19 December 1968 to establish a Special Committee to investigate Israeli practices affecting the population of the Occupied Territories. Twenty-one years later, the terms of reference of the Committee were changed to investigate Israeli practices concerning the human rights of the Palestinian people and other Arabs in the Occupied Territories.

The Committee, after exhaustive investigation, reported that "...the Government of Israel continued to withhold its co-operation from the Special Committee." On the basis of information and first-hand evidence that it was able to collect, the Committee reported that "...the situation in the occupied territories has been marked by a dangerous level of violence and repression, which has constantly escalated since the start of the uprising of the Palestinian population against occupation in December 1987." It asserted that during the period under consideration, Israel continued to follow its policy of annexing the occupied territories. The report runs into several pages. It mentions the raids that Israel carried out to collect tax, to arrest suspects and demolish houses. It declares: "Numerous cases of severe beating and the breaking of bones, casualties provoked by tear-gas and rock throwing into houses or other confined areas such as mosques or schools ... have been reported to the Committee...." The dead and casualty figures of teenagers under 16 and babies, who were killed by gunfire and burning, were also reported.[85]

On several occasions, Israel had breached the UN resolution 3452 (XXX) adopted by the General Assembly on 9 December 1975, regarding protection of all persons from being subjected to torture and other cruel, inhuman or degrading treatment or punishment.

Chapter 8 : Torture and War Crimes

On 3 December 1973, resolution 3074 [XXVIII] was passed by the General Assembly, on the Principles of International co-operation in the detection, arrest, extradition and punishment of persons guilty of war crimes and crimes against humanity. It declares: "War crimes and crimes against humanity, wherever they are committed shall be subject to investigation and the persons against whom there is evidence that they have committed such crimes shall be subject to tracing, arrest, trial and, if found guilty, to punishment."[86]

The Law Society in Jerusalem has been warning that extrajudicial assassinations and killing of bystanders by the Israeli forces are war crimes under Article 8 of the Rome Statute of the International Criminal Court. It is calling for investigation of these criminal offences under the Fourth Geneva Convention and for trial under the International Court of Justice.[87]

Amnesty International and Human Rights Watch jointly addressed an appeal to the leaders of the US, EU, Israel and UN Secretary-General Kofi Annan, in which, they stressed the need to send international human rights monitors to the West Bank and Gaza. They warned that civilians have been the primary victims of the systematic human rights violations. They emphasized how their own reported violations and recommendations had been incorporated in the Mitchell Report and George Tenet cease-fire plan. Yet, in the absence of international observers to monitor both sides, the Mitchell and Tenet plans remained merely ink on paper. The letter reflected on the killing of Palestinian civilians at checkpoints and preventing them from reaching 'urgent medical care'.[88]

This has become a daily occurrence and a common feature in the West Bank and Gaza. Israel is quite confident that the appeal of humanitarian agencies will be ignored in as much as the earlier appeals of the UN Human Rights chief, Mary Robinson were ignored. Dangerous precedents have already been laid down due to the UN impotence.

If the perpetrators of the dreadful crimes of Sabra and Shatila could get away from prosecution, then this was tantamount to sending a message that any crimes committed against the

Chapter 8 : Torture and War Crimes

Palestinians enjoy immunity from accountability. The dreadful scenes of massacre at the Palestinian refugee camps of Sabra and Shatila in Lebanon were relayed around the globe by the world media. The world was shocked to see the indiscriminate killing of women and children. But nothing has changed for decades. No one has yet been indicted by the United Nations War Crimes Tribunal for crimes against humanity in the refugee camps..

There is a principle in international law that in addition to those who carry out crimes, "criminal liability will also accrue to any political or military superior who orders, colludes in, condones, or fails to take steps to prevent their commission..."[89] In the aftermath of the Sabra and Shatila massacre, there was widespread condemnation at international level. The people of Israel feared reprisals. The public chose to disassociate itself from the actions of the commanders on the field. There was a large demonstration in Tel Aviv. There was no other option for the government of Israel but to appoint a commission of inquiry to look into the matter.

The inquiry was held similar to the inquiry in the wake of My Lai massacre of 1968 in Vietnam by the US army. In the aftermath of the My Lai massacre, international condemnation of US actions in Vietnam and student demonstrations in the US compelled the authorities to act. The captain in the US army, Ernest Medina, alleged to have issued the order to massacre 200 Vietnamese civilians in March 1968, was court-martialled. The commander confessed that he learnt about the massacre but decided to cover up the event and did not take any step to report the massacre to his superiors. Therefore, the charge of premeditated murder could not be proved. On a lesser charge of involuntary manslaughter, the captain was held not guilty and was acquitted.[90] All other senior officers who were brought to trial in connection with the massacre of civilians were found not guilty.

There was a striking similarity between the outcome of the trial of the My Lai massacre and that of Sabra and Shatila. The Commission of Inquiry set up by the government of Israel reported its outcome. The Kahan Report concluded: "...It was the duty of the Minister of Defence [Ariel Sharon] to take into account all the

Chapter 8 : Torture and War Crimes

reasonable considerations for and against having the Phalangists enter the camps..." Sharon was pre-warned about the hatred and vengeful conduct of the Phalangists towards the Palestinians. Yet, his forces provided all the facilities to enable them to enter the civilian camps.

The report continued: "...[Sharon] made a grave mistake when he ignored the danger of acts of revenge and bloodshed by the Phalangists against the population in the refugee camps. ...Responsibility is to be imputed to the Minister of Defence for having disregarded the danger...and for having failed to take this danger into account ...[and] for not ordering appropriate measures for preventing or reducing the danger of massacre. ...The blunders constitute the non-fulfillment of a duty with which the Defence Minister was charged.[91] Having made these observations, the Commission decided that Sharon was not in any way responsible for the massacre. It negated all its findings. It seemed that the judicial inquiry was initiated to quash bad publicity that Israeli policies in Lebanon had attracted. But the conclusion had to succumb to political dictates. Therefore, like the perpetrators of My Lai massacre, those responsible for the Sabra and Shatila slaughter were not made accountable for their crimes.

The *Naval War College Review*, 1997, observes that the Kahan Commission absolved Sharon from all responsibility for his failure, although he was in a position of knowing that a massacre was a certainty. It continues that the decision was on "purely political grounds" as the Commission was concerned about the negative impact on the Israelis if a Defence Minister was to be charged with criminal negligence in failing to stop the massacre.

Then the NWC Review makes most the important legal point under international law that as per the Commission's investigatory report, "there was enough evidence to indict Sharon for failure as a commander to prevent the commission of war crimes or crimes against humanity, and certainly for offences under the national Criminal Code..." But Israeli courts neither applied the national law nor international law to indict Sharon.

Robert Fisk in his excellent article[92] reflects that Sharon, like

Chapter 8 : Torture and War Crimes

the French generals in Algeria, massacred the Arabs. He writes: "It needed an Israeli writer...to point out that Sharon's career spells anything but peace. He voted against the peace treaty with Egypt in 1979. He voted against a withdrawal from southern Lebanon in 1985. He opposed Israel's participation in the Madrid peace conference in 1991. He opposed the Knesset plenum vote on the Oslo agreement in 1993. He abstained on a vote for peace with Jordan in 1994. He voted against the Hebron agreement in 1997. ..." The article goes on to identify how Sharon's career is built against peace. In the latest 'road map', he has recorded fourteen reservations. But he urges the Palestinians to implement the 'road map' without any reservations. His constant effort to frustrate any peace effort has cost the lives of the Israeli and Palestinian civilians.

BBC TV programme *Panorama* on 17 June 2001, explored Ariel Sharon's role in the Sabra and Shatila massacre.[93] Immediately after appearing on the programme, Professor Richard Falk, who is Jewish, received threats from Sharon's supporters, and was put under police protection. He said on *Panorama*: "There is absolutely no question in my mind that he [Sharon] is indictable for the knowledge he had or should have had." The Professor, an expert in international law, was a former member of an international commission that looked into the massacre of the Palestinian refugees. He further asserted: "Sharon's specific command responsibility arises from the fact that he was Minister of Defence in touch with the field commanders, that he actually was present then in Beirut, that he met with the Phalange leadership, and it was he that gave the directions and orders that resulted in the Phalange entering the camps..."

Apart from Sabra and Shatila, Sharon has been named as directly responsible for the earlier Qibya massacre. The survivors of the massacre believe that they have all the right to seek redress under international law. They took this unresolved matter to a Belgian court to indict him on the basis of the law allowing criminal trials for war crimes, regardless of where they take place.[94]

The complaint in the Belgian court was launched under a law of 1993, which states that Belgian courts can try human rights violations and atrocities even if non-Belgians committed them

Chapter 8 : Torture and War Crimes

outside the country. But this attempt too by the aggrieved families has been thwarted under pressure from America. Justice has become a rare commodity in the civilized world. Israel broke diplomatic relations with Belgium over this law. Donald Rumsfeld at a press conference in Brussels threatened Belgium that it risked, what he called, "losing its status" to "host NATO's headquarters if it did not rescind the law". Human Rights Watch said that Rumsfeld was wrong to threaten the Belgians.[95] But Brussels succumbed to the American pressure and the government decided to repeal the law altogether.

Politicization of justice is the most abhorrent trend that is witnessed in present-day politics. In this way, the international justice system is subjected to mockery. Audacious war criminals can put up a brave face and move around the world capitals with freedom, so long as they have a backing in one or the other seats of power. Several examples can be cited to prove this point. During the separation of East and West Germany, a shoot-to-kill order was issued against anyone trying to cross the border through the Berlin Wall. After the reunification, Eric Honecker, the Head of State of the German Democratic Republic from 1976 to 1989 was charged for the crime of issuing such orders, as a result of which, 800 East Germans had been killed. Heinz Kessler, the former Defence Minister and other members of the East German Defence Council and six former East German generals were also tried. Green writes that the "very small cogs" in the chain of command could not escape custodial sentences. Whereas, the "big cog", Eric Honecker himself was discharged because of his cancer. He was released to join his family in Chile, where it was disclosed that the cancer he was suffering from was not serious.[96]

A somewhat new political philosophy came to light against surrendering General Augusto Pinochet, the former dictator of Chile, to stand trial in Spain for the disappearance and torture of political dissidents. The very legality of his arrest on UK soil was questioned because in his heydays he had been an ally of Britain. Does this mean that if dictators in their heydays had been enemies of Britain, politicians would have interpreted international Protocols differently?

Dual standards in respect of dispensation of justice against war criminals are bound to frustrate the international judicial system. After the war in Afghanistan and Iraq, the US was deeply concerned about a range of lawsuits that could arise against its military and political officials. Therefore, the Bush Administration rescinded President Clinton's signature to the treaty establishing the International Criminal Court. According to Leopold, this means that "U.S. citizens and contract workers [will be] out of the reach of the court".[97]

The US pressurized the former republics of Yugoslavia - Slovenia, Bosnia, Croatia, Serbia and Macedonia, to join 39 other countries around the globe in granting immunity to the Americans for war crimes. It campaigned that the Balkan states should cooperate with the War Crimes Tribunal at The Hague, but not with the International Criminal Court. *The Guardian* writes: "Washington is vehemently opposed to the permanent international criminal court..." It threatened the Balkan states with boycott of economic aid if the Americans were not exempted from accountability for war crimes. Human Rights Watch called the attempt, a 'blatant hypocrisy'.

The European Union issued counter-ultimatum that if the former east European states succumbed to the US threats, they would prejudice their application to join the EU.[98] Washington has stopped aid to 35 countries, including ten African countries that refused to surrender to its pressure for absolving the Americans from the jurisdiction of the international criminal court. The White House spokesman Ari Fleischer declared: "It's important to protect American service men and women and others in government." What he would not declare is that if all the nations start believing that their governments are above the law and should be exempt from any prosecution, then the world would plummet into the law of the jungle.

9

Genocides – Heinous Crimes against Humanity

THE United Nations updated the Geneva Conventions of 1949 by protocols, which were adopted by the General Assembly on 9 December 1970 (GA resolution 2675 [XXV]).[99]

It ratified fundamental human rights accepted in international law (para 1). It specified: "In the conduct of military operations during armed conflicts, a distinction must be made at all times between persons actively taking part in the hostilities and civilian populations" (para 2)."...[E]very effort should be made to spare civilian populations from the ravages of war, and all necessary precaution should be taken to avoid injury, loss or damage to civilian populations" (para 3). It is astounding how these provisions are breached when human rights clash with the political interests of powerful nations.

The key clause of GA resolution reads: "Civilian population or individual members thereof should not be the object of reprisals, forcible transfers or other assaults on their integrity" (para 7). Ever since the loss of the Palestinian homeland, Israel has persistently contravened this clause. Sharon's reservations against the return of refugees to their homes would be one of the stumbling-blocks that would certainly vitiate the 'road map'.

The UN Convention against Genocide consisting of 19 Articles declared that genocide, conspiracy or incitement to commit genocide is all illegal. Individuals are to be held responsible for these acts whether they were acting in their official capacities or as private individuals. (UN General Assembly Resolution 260A III, passed on 9 December 1948). After the US government of the time betrayed the mass uprising against Saddam in 1991, he uprooted the entire marshland in the South of Iraq. He destroyed the culture and way of life that had prevailed for thousands of years. He poisoned the waters of the marshes and massacred hundreds of thousands of the inhabitants. This was one of the worst genocides of the twentieth century that has gone unpunished.

Brief extracts highlight the principal clauses of the Convention. Clause A1: "Genocide, whether committed in time of peace or in time of war, is a crime under international law." Clause A11: "In the present Convention, genocide means any of the following acts committed with intent to destroy, in whole or in part, a national, ethnical, racial or religious group, such as: (a) killing members of the group, (b) causing serious bodily or mental harm to members of the group, (c) deliberately inflicting on the group conditions of life calculated to bring about its physical destruction in whole or in part".

Genocide in Cambodia

The genocide of Pol Pot and his Khmer Rouge, the Cambodian guerrilla group, left a black legacy of Communism in the twentieth century. The country's social, cultural, economic and religious lives were categorically destroyed. In what was to become one of the worst killing machines, between one and two million Cambodians were annihilated through monstrous cruelty. Their remains were unearthed in 1980. Even children were tortured and killed. Pol Pot was a Paris-educated evil intellectual. He took control of the country in 1975, and with the fanatical support of the Khmer Rouge, embarked upon a bloodbath. Ten million land-mines were left behind to continue maiming the population of Cambodia.

Genocide in Rwanda

Africa is the poorest continent in the world, not because it has no natural and human resources. To the contrary, it has some of the richest resources in the world. But the overwhelming majority of the people are uneducated and programmed by their corrupt leaders to engage in ethnic rivalries and hostilities. The extreme manifestation of this was Rwanda in the last decade of the twentieth century.

Chapter 9: Genocides – Heinous Crimes against Humanity

One of the poorest countries in East-Central Africa, Rwanda was divided into three main tribes: 84 percent Hutu, 14 percent Tutsi and others, 2 percent. Despite being in the minority, the Tutsi had dominated the country economically and politically for over 500 years. In 1959, Tutsi domination ended. Since then, conflict between the two ethnic groups has continued, and was aggravated by propaganda warfare which culminated in the massacre of 1994.

The Hutus were waiting for any pretext to unleash their rage against the Tutsi. They got their ammunition to ignite the fire of civil war when the plane of their President Habyarimana was shot down on 6 April 1994. The terrifying massacre that followed resulted in attacks with iron bars, machetes and axes. Churches, schools, hospitals, orphanages and civilian abodes of refuge were attacked mercilessly. Women, children, infants, babies and the disabled were subjected to an indiscriminate murdering spree. In a mere one hundred days, up to a million men, women and children were massacred.

Within a week of the President's death, the gangsters of the Presidential Guard had killed 20,000 Tutsis. Mutilated bodies filled the streets, some of them were cut into pieces. In Kibuye, 15,000 Tutsis were rounded up in a stadium and massacred.

A report published in *African Rights* wrote that women had played an active role in the killings of men and women. The barbarity and cruelty displayed by women in the Rwandan civil war was unprecedented. Nurses supplied lists of patients to be killed. Some women killed small children with their own hands. The Rwandan situation was at the apex of disasters, worsened by blind hatred and vengeful emotions.

The Rwandan civil war created one of the largest refugee crises on the continent. All the surviving girls had been raped. Wartime pregnancies reached 5,000. On 8 November 1994, The International Tribunal for Rwanda was established under Chapter VII of the Charter of the United Nations, to prosecute individuals responsible for genocide and other serious violations of international law.

Five weeks after the commencement of genocide, the UN

Chapter 9: Genocides – Heinous Crimes against Humanity

imposed an arms embargo on Rwanda on 17 May 1994. Despite the embargo, Gilbert writes, "a British firm had supplied the Hutu with a considerable quantity of arms...." He continues: "The first shipment, of almost a million rounds of ammunition, valued at $750,000 had been flown from Israel, as had the second shipment, of more than a million rounds of ammunition and the ten thousand grenades. ...The British firm had organized the shipments, and made its customary profit from them, as had the Israeli firms involved.[100]

The CNN reported on 22 August 2001, that official memorandums issued by the Pentagon and by Warren Christopher, the then Secretary of State in May 1994, indicated that within a few days, the Clinton Administration became aware of the Genocide in Rwanda. And yet, nothing was done to stop it under military action.

The UK Foreign and Commonwealth Office reports: "War crimes are serious violations of the laws and customs of war, such as ill-treatment of prisoners of war or deliberate targeting of civilians. Crimes against humanity are serious crimes committed as part of a widespread or systematic attack directly against a civilian population."[101]

Nalini Lalla, wrote on the *Womenaid International* web page that 100,000 accused were waiting to be tried by the local Rwandan courts. In a country where there were only sixteen practising defence lawyers and judges had only six months' training, doubts were expressed by the human rights groups on the credibility of the trials. She expressed her serious concern that as the death penalty is recognized by Rwandan laws, many innocent people may end up on the gallows. On the other hand, where trials are held by UN Tribunals, most of the guilty, if ever caught, would get prison sentences.

It was however, common knowledge that Rwanda was not in a position to organize the administration of justice through fair and impartial trials. There was no space in the jails to accommodate 100,000 accused of war crimes. There was an inherent danger of leaving the conduct of trial to mob prosecution. Those who had lost members of their family or were themselves suffering from the trauma of rape would have been inclined to take revenge against their rival tribe members. Expediency in such cases would be mistaken for justice, in which case, the axe was likely to fall on the neck of many innocent victims who could not defend themselves. The only just and fair way to deal with this humanitarian problem was for the United Nations War Crimes Tribunal to take full charge, including the cost involved in administrating these trials. But this was unlikely to happen.

Genocide in Bosnia and Kosovo

In the opening years of the twentieth century, the history of the Balkans gave all the indications that centuries old rivalries and cruel ethnic hatred were on the way to being revived on a larger scale. On 31 August 1903, shocking atrocities were reported from the Balkans, where whole villages were put to the sword, women were raped and small children were bayoneted.[102]

As the century progressed, the 'superpowers' openly violated the rules of warfare. Small nations followed the precedents laid down by the 'superpowers'. Acts of revenge knew no bounds. No distinction was drawn between parties directly involved and the civilians caught up in the conflict. A need was felt to devise regulatory rules to save civilians from brutalities during and after the wars. Deliberations at international level took place and legal opinion in regard to the command responsibility was also laid down.

The conventions that had been adopted at the Hague Peace Conference of 1899 and 1907 in relation to the violators, specifically provided that "…the offending parties should be punished, after a judicial hearing,…[they] are liable to the punishment specified in the penal law. …"[103]

When the conventions were implemented in practice, a vital precedent was set in the trial of General Yamashita in 1946. The President of the Military Commission declared: "…Where murder and rape and vicious, revengeful actions are widespread offences, and there is no effective attempt by a commander to discover and control the criminal acts, such a commander may be held responsible, or even criminally liable, for the lawless acts of his troops. ..."[104]

Another important precedent was established in the German High Command Trial of 1948. It was held that the soldiers, engaged on the ground in pillage and the destruction of civilian life and property, and killing of prisoners of war, could not plead that they were acting upon the command of their superiors. The criterion should be that the order given is criminal or one which is known to be criminal. The criminality may be deduced from the act itself that is forbidden by international agreements or is 'inherently criminal' and contrary to 'accepted principles of humanity'.[105] There were hence, adequate legal precedents and judgements to indict later on, the Serb leaders and commanders for the worst atrocities in Europe since World War II.

On 3 July 2001, the first Head of State faced the United Nations War Crimes Tribunal at The Hague for his part in crimes against humanity in Kosovo. The arrest and trial of Slobodan Milosevic will never be able to undo the ruins and devastation caused to the lives of the victims. The heinous crimes committed by the Serbs in Bosnia, Croatia and Kosovo, in the name of Serb nationalistic fascism will retain indelible scars in the memory of the survivors.

The demonstrations by the ultra-nationalists in Belgrade, in protest against the arrest of Milosevic, reflected their confession that their leaders had committed crimes against humanity on their behalf. Hence, in their thinking, the surrender of an indicted war criminal was an insult to national pride, the pride which would leave nothing to be proud of in the history of the Balkan wars.

Only a year after his attempt to annul the popular vote against him in the general election, Milosevic had to be handed over to The Hague Tribunal. Though his initial charges were crimes against humanity committed in Kosovo, the indictment was extended for his part in the crimes committed in Croatia and Bosnia. He refused to recognize the legality of the Tribunal, not that it would make any difference to how the trial was to be conducted. A not guilty plea was entered on his behalf. It seemed certain that Milosevic and his legal advisers were under the impression that a

Chapter 9: Genocides – Heinous Crimes against Humanity

Head of State can never be extradited to face a trial at The Hague. Had they done their homework, they would have discovered that The Statute of the International Tribunal for the Prosecution of Persons Responsible for Serious Violations of International Humanitarian Law committed in the Territory of the former Yugoslavia since 1991, specifically provided that:

1 "A person who planned, instigated, ordered, committed or otherwise ordered and abetted in the planning, preparation and execution of a crime [listed in the Statute], shall be individually responsible for the crime."

2 "The official position of any accused person, whether as Head of State or Government or as a responsible Government official, shall not relieve such person of criminal responsibility nor mitigate punishment. ..."

In the aftermath of World War II, the Allied Powers issued a statement asserting the need to punish through a proper judicial system "those guilty of these crimes, whether they have ordered them, perpetrated them, or participated in them."[106] The most important point to note is that the London (Nuremberg) Charter did not exempt even the Head of State responsible for war crimes from prosecution.

The two other chief war criminals wanted by the tribunal are Radovan Karadzic and Ratko Mladic. Karadzic was a general in the Bosnian Serb armed forces, commander of the Bosnian Serb army and president of the Serbian Democratic Party in the former Socialist Republic of Bosnia and Herzegovina. Mladic was a corps commander in the Yugoslav People's Army in Croatia and commanded the army of the Bosnian Serb administration. Both were indicted for their direct role in genocide, crimes against humanity, deportation of civilians, unlawful confinement and destruction of sacred sites.[107] They are yet to be extradited to stand trial.

The Russian moral and military support of the Serb aggressors in Bosnia was instrumental in prolonging the Balkan war in the last decade of the twentieth century. Whatever action the West decided to take in Kosovo in the late 1990s, was too little too late. A timely action against the Serbs in Bosnia would have saved more than 200,000 innocent Muslim civilians from cold-blooded genocide.

If the Serb expansionist ambition had been contained a decade ago, the disaster that befell the Kosovans would have been totally avoided. Ethnic cleansing was the cause and effect of several identifiable factors. Europe was not interested in stopping its dirtiest war in the Balkans until the cost was phenomenal in terms of human life. The United States and the United Nations failed to lift the unjust arms embargo on Bosnia for self-defence. The secretariat of the United Nations failed to overcome its indifferent attitude towards the crisis. The Owen–Vance mission dragged on and on at an enormous human cost.

Boutros Boutros-Ghali, the Secretary-General of the United Nations at that time, took the trouble to travel only once to Sarajevo, the centre of one of the major crises of the twentieth century. On 31 December 1992, he called the war in the Balkans "a rich man's war." Whether it was a rich man's war or a poor man's war, the main concern of a person in his shoes, should have been to bring an end to it. Instead, he went on to remark, "…you have a situation that is better than ten other places in the world…I can give you a list." This was not the time to demonstrate one's expertise in international crises. The UN Secretary-General offered some consolation and no commitment to the victims of genocide. He was telling them that they should not be building any hopes; after all, they were eleventh in the order of priority.

David Rieff writes: "…Long after the Bosnian Serb forces had expelled from the valleys of eastern Bosnia most of their former majority of Muslim inhabitants, and long after the over-whelming majority of the mosques of northern Bosnia had been blown up, thus eliminating the traces of a European Islam that had existed in the region for five centuries, President Clinton presided over the opening of the Holocaust Museum in Washington, D.C. …He did have one suggestion …So that the genocide that befell European Jewry during the Nazi period never take place again."[108]

As the crises took draconian toll on civilian lives, and as the plight of the refugees was putting a heavy burden on the resources of

Chapter 9: Genocides – Heinous Crimes against Humanity

the European nations, it became difficult for NATO to maintain its 'wait and see' attitude. When the crisis extended to Kosovo in the late 1990s, the West decided to activate NATO forces under a mandate from the United Nations.

For the first time in the history of Europe, the Serb forces had used mass-rape of Muslim women in Bosnia as the main weapon of war. The frightening accounts of the victims published in the international press provided an insight into the sick minds and deranged thinking of the Serbian war criminals at work.

Hatred mongering and racist-nationalism had manifested itself in the Serb conduct from the early days of the Balkan war. On 13 March 1994, when the UN observers entered the Serb-controlled enclave in Bosnia, they found that 20,000 inhabitants were in a state of starvation.

The Times of London wrote: "On July 11, 1995…in Srebrenica, a UN 'safe area', an estimated 7,000 men and boys – 12,000 is the figure sometimes quoted – disappeared into a forest seeking refuge from the Serb advance."[109] Madeleine Albright, the US Secretary of State in the Clinton Administration, was taken to see the mass graves which were uncovered near Srebrenica. She described what she saw: "It is the most disgusting and horrifying sight for another human being to see".

In his well-researched book,[110] David Rohde presents compelling and convincing evidence of complicity in the massacre, between the United Nations commander of the 'safe area' and the war criminal, General Ratko Mladic. Rohde blames US and UN negligence for the disaster. The French General Bernard Janvier, who was the senior UN commander, refused the deployment of the NATO force to protect the unarmed civilians.

The megalomaniac Ratko Mladic considered the Dutch peacekeepers as his 'prisoners'. Rohde writes: "The action of the Clinton Administration and its allies aided, encouraged, and emboldened the executions" of thousands of Muslim civilians. Some Dutch peacekeepers were racists. They later on testified that they hated Muslims. He continues: "Dutch observation posts…began falling like dominos. …The Dutch were despondent and put up no resistance. ...In the end, being a Bosnian Serb hostage was paradise compared with being a peacekeeper." A Dutch soldier was quoted as saying: " 'The Serbs treated me very well. We could take a shower if we wanted. ...We could play soccer and basketball. Three meals a day. Cigarettes and beer...' "[111]

Before dispatching the peacekeepers to the war zone, the UN should have cautioned them that they were not going there for a picnic. But the UN and NATO were negligent, as a result of which, they risked the lives of thousands who were slaughtered mercilessly.

Before and after the takeover of Srebrenica, it was obvious that the Dutch peacekeepers' ineptitude would pave the way for disaster. The Serbs had made no secret of their pathological fury against the Muslims. Several days after abandoning their posts and after the massacre of Srebrenica, the Dutch commander had said that they had no evidence of war crimes and that 'a correct military operation' was carried out in 'the right way'.

The savagery of the Serbs knew no bounds. In order to capture Muslim men fleeing Srebrenica, they poisoned water in a stream near the town of Konjevic Polje. This was not the first time they had poisoned wells.[112] Several years after the genocide, the grim faces of the grief-stricken survivors spoke volumes about the trauma they had suffered.[113] The perpetrators of mass-rape did not give any value to the dignity of women.

The NATO officers left the war criminals to roam around Bosnia for years after they had committed their atrocities. They arrogantly refused to safeguard the Serbs' next victims in Kosovo.[114] Those who engineered war crimes went ahead in occupying the land and houses of the expelled inhabitants. Instead of remorse, they rewarded themselves with the booty of war. The victims felt that the criminals who were directly involved in the atrocities and their commanders must be arrested and brought to justice. Otherwise, the history of the Balkans would have a fairytale-like outcome that the Serbs, who killed, burned, plundered, raped and displaced people from their homes, ended up building, developing, flourishing and living happily thereafter.

On 29 November 1996, the United Nations War Crimes

Chapter 9: Genocides – Heinous Crimes against Humanity

Tribunal at The Hague sentenced 24-year-old Drazen Erdemovic, a Bosnian Serb soldier, after he confessed to killing at least 70 unarmed Muslims. He was given a ten-year sentence by a French judge, Claude Jorda because the killer showed 'remorse' and testified against other war criminals. The sentence was a joke and mockery of justice. The convict was the first person to be tried and sentenced by the international tribunal since the German and Japanese war criminals were hanged at the end of World War II.[115]

The first trial of its kind of systematic rape and sexual enslavement of Bosnian Muslim women by Bosnian Serbs started on 20 March 2000 and ended on 22 February 2001 at The Hague. A guilty verdict against the three Serb soldiers was a consolation, but not recompense to the victims. Nothing could possibly compensate for the mental and physical torments that the victims had suffered in a state of total helplessness. Thousands of Muslim women and girls, as young as 12 years, were picked up by these beasts from their concentration camps and were subjected to gang rapes.

The presiding judge, Florence Mumba, said that the defendants had "thrived in the dark atmosphere of the dehumanization of those believed to be enemies". Sixteen rape victims testified and unravelled their terrifying experiences. The men were guilty, in the words of the judge, of "nightmarish scheme of sexual exploitation." The judge told one of the accused: "You abused and ravaged Muslim women because of their ethnicity, and from among their number you picked whosoever you fancied."

Among the war criminals there was a woman who had been received and welcomed by several heads of state. A detailed profile[116] of the 'Iron Lady' of the Balkans, Biljana Plavsic, the former Bosnian Serb President, gives a rare insight into a polluted human mind. She approved of ethnic cleansing and showed great appreciation for the Serb war criminals, who tortured and raped Muslim women. She called Muslims "genetically deformed". She faced charges of complicity in the mass-massacre, execution, beating, torture, deportation and destruction of the civilian population of Bosnia. The war in the Balkans left demographic damage to the life in Bosnia and later on, in Kosovo.

Chapter 9: Genocides – Heinous Crimes against Humanity

On 31 July 2001, a Bosnian Serb, Stevan Todorovic the former police chief who admitted to committing rapes, torture and murders between 1992 and 1993 near the border of Bosnia Herzegovina and Croatia received a ten-year sentence. Again, the sentence was a complete joke. The War Crimes Tribunal was extraordinarily compassionate because the accused had 'cooperated' with the authorities by admitting his crimes. It was indeed very kind of the accused and therefore, he had to be rewarded.

The Judge Patrick Robinson said, his crimes were "particularly grave". But he had taken into consideration his guilty plea and his remorse. How was the so-called 'remorse' so precisely being measured? Was he placed in a similar situation and turned his head away? Or perhaps he said 'sorry' and that was quite adequate. The lucky murderer will once again enjoy freedom, which he had ruthlessly denied to his victims. Before killing them, he had also compelled them to perform certain detestable acts, while his perverted psyche enjoyed the scene. How can society be safe with these types of dangerous criminals around?

On 2 August 2001, the former Bosnian Serb general, Radislav Kristic was sentenced to 46 years for his part in the genocide in Srebrenica in July 1995, after the enclave of shelter was declared a 'safe haven' under the UN protection. The ethnic cleansing of between 7,000-8,000 Bosnian Muslim men and boys was carried out right under the nose of UN Dutch observers, and perhaps under their supervision and consent.

The Srebrenica massacre was officially recognized by the presiding judge as the first case of genocide after World War II. Kristic was the most important war criminal to be tried after the Nazis. At the age of 96, it will still be possible for this criminal to be released from prison and live a normal life. But the legacy of permanent affliction that he and his superiors, Radovan Karadzic and Ratko Mladic have left on the surviving victims will not be forgotten.

The very least that could be done to console the survivors of the disaster is that those who are convicted of genocide should be left to rot in prison and never see freedom again. Their victims begged to be killed, but they preferred to leave them in agony through the nights, before unleashing a dreadful murdering spree on them. The big sharks in the crime of genocide are Radovan Karadzic and Ratko Mladic who have not yet been brought to justice. If the US and Europe were determined, they could have imposed biting economic sanctions on the new government to compel it to surrender these war criminals to The Hague.

On the subject of the prisoners of conscience in the Republic of Yugoslavia, Amnesty International report of 2001 declares: "Hundreds of ethnic Albanian prisoners transferred from Kosovo when Serbian and Yugoslav forces withdrew were sentenced to prison terms after unfair trials. ...At least 3,300 people remained unaccounted for in Kosovo" up to the end of 2000.

These Albanian prisoners were tried as 'terrorists'. The evidence presented against them was flimsy and circumstantial. Several instances were cited in the report of unfair trials, confessions obtained under torture, and the violation of international standards while sentencing them. In one case, where the sentence of a prisoner of conscience was overturned by the Supreme Military Court in Belgrade, the case was reverted to the Military Court for retrial.

On the conditions in Bosnia, Amnesty International Report 2001 states that the Serb secondary school students protested against sharing education facilities with Bosnian students. This racist sentiment against the Bosnian returnees, whose shops were vandalized and whose houses were set on fire in Srebrenica, added insult to injury. The report says that according to the International Committee of the Red Cross, more than 17,500 people are unaccounted for, and more than 4,000 remains were exhumed. The report adds: "In Sultanovici...a plot of land holding four mass graves and containing 300 bodies was used...as a rubbish dump for more than six months".

Chapter 9: Genocides – Heinous Crimes against Humanity

Genocide in Chechnya

The human tragedy that befell the people of Chechnya through Russian heavy artillery raids was another incident of genocide in modern history. Despite dreadful scenes of indiscriminate killings of the aged, women and children, the international community demonstrated its lack of will to face the challenge posed by Russian aggression. The Russian propaganda machinery projected success, because the air raids and the policy of mass destruction did the dirty job for them. Their land mines trapped helpless civilians and tore them apart. They bombed non-military targets to uproot the natives from their land. It was without doubt, an act of genocide engineered by a permanent member of the Security Council.

The unjust system of permanent membership on the Security Council and the power of veto that the members enjoy, have more often than not, helped to prolong human suffering. The aggressors were confident that the West would make some haphazard noises of protest followed by inaction.

Vladimir Putin's invasion of Chechnya displaced a third of the population, more than 260,000 people within Chechnya and another 170,000 were condemned to live in difficult circumstances. Putin presented his campaign as a war against 'Islamic Fundamentalism'. Later on he was to solicit the support of China and India to crack down on their Muslim minorities.[117]

According to Human Rights Watch, the Russian authorities have buried the evidence of extra judicial executions in Chechnya. The 24-page comprehensive report was released on 15 May 2001 under the title 'Burying the Evidence: The Botched Investigation into a Mass Grave in Chechnya'.

It is certainly not coincidental that on his visit to Belgrade, prior to Milosevic's arrest, Putin promised an economic aid package to the new government. He made a point that Russian economic assistance would be unconditional. The implication was that it was not conditional to the surrender of Milosevic to The Hague to face trial. His sympathy for a person indicted of war crimes and crimes against humanity, was quite understandable because his own troops and commanders in Chechnya sailed in the same boat.

Russia wanted a quick and hushed-up solution to the political crisis in Chechnya but the world media and Human Rights groups exposed the Russian crimes. How can a power so deeply engrossed in flagrant violation of the UN resolutions be trusted to shoulder responsibility in solving global crises as a member of the Security Council?

From 19 March through 27 April 2001, the UN Commission of Human Rights held its meeting in Geneva and asked its members to condemn Russian atrocities and recommended establishing an international commission of inquiry. Human Rights Watch reported summary executions, disappearance of civilians, torture, widespread destruction and looting and discovery of mass gravesites in Chechnya.

On 24 February 2001, the remains of fifty-one people were found in a mass grave. They were seen alive in Russian custody, which means, no trials and no convictions had taken place before executing them. They were in civilian clothing, and some were blindfolded. Many had their hands and feet tied up. The site where the graves were uncovered had been under Russian military control since the invasion in 1999.

The Russian government was not interested in co-operating to preserve crucial evidence, which would have helped identify the perpetrators of these crimes. This shows the extent to which there had been an official cover-up. Earlier, eight mass graves were found, where the bodies bore the signs of torture. Human Rights Watch posted detailed eye-witness reports of the survivors, whose missing relatives were killed and dumped.

In its leader article, *The Guardian* writes: "A halt to Vladimir Putin's criminal war against the Chechen people is long overdue. Even the Russian president cannot any longer pretend that his policy of suppression and annihilation is working. ...6500 Russian servicemen have died and at least 20,000 have been injured. Civilian casualties are in the uncounted tens of thousands...human rights are flouted on a tragic scale."[118] Neither the International Monetary Fund nor the World Bank had been given any signal by Washington to link further loans to Russia with its human rights records.

The *Associated Press* reported on 11 July 2001, that General Vladimir Moltenskoi, Russia's top military commander in Chechnya said that his troops had committed crimes against civilians during the searches for rebels, and promised to seek the population's forgiveness. The General said that large-scale crimes had been committed similar to the Tatar invasion that devastated Russia in the thirteenth century.

Of course, seeking forgiveness has no basis in international law, which provides that the war criminals must be arrested, tried and punished. This is what the civilians, who fled their own country to become refugees, and the human rights groups, would like to have seen.

The Russian government has been successful in banning foreign reporters from Chechnya to black out the news. Patrick Cockburn writes: "The war in Chechnya is of extraordinary savagery, just as bad as anything which happened in Kosovo. Torture and disappearances are routine. The best parallel with what is happening here is the French war in Algeria."[119] The article highlights grim facts that the Russian soldiers and officials who have not been paid their salaries, engage in kidnapping the villagers, and extorting money from them.

Amnesty International Report 2001 spells out the gross violation of human rights in Chechnya. "Serious and widespread human rights violations...including grave crimes against civilians on a massive scale" were committed. "Russian federal forces were responsible", says the report. "Thousands of civilians were killed in indiscriminate attacks and there were widespread reports of torture ...and summary executions." The complicity on the part of Russian officials in fuelling public sentiments against the Chechens has been highlighted. "The Russian authorities repeatedly made inflammatory statements designed to divert public criticism of the government by heightening anti-Chechen sentiments in the country", the report adds. This provocative policy was to result in terrible radical reaction on the other side.

Under the grisly situation in Chechnya, the report states that

Chapter 9: Genocides – Heinous Crimes against Humanity

even the medical personnel were not spared. The 'cleansing operation' continued and women and children who had been promised safe passage came under artillery attack. Prisoners were being beaten with truncheons and tortured. There were numerous cases of, according to the report, "detainees being raped, beaten with hammers and clubs, and given electric shocks or tear gassed." The 2001 report makes a distressed reading. It exposes some shocking facts: "There were also reports that some detainees had their teeth filed down or were beaten around both ears...to burst the eardrums." Eye-witness statements were presented, indicating that a 14-year-old girl and a 16-year-old boy were gang raped by the Russian prison guards. This type of monstrous conduct was an invitation to the Chechen groups to respond with violence, which brought grim consequences for both the Russians and the Chechens.

Amnesty states that there are an estimated 300,000 civilians who remain displaced. It says, "reports continued to be received that in some cases police fabricated criminal charges against Chechens and planted drugs or weapons on them."

The Russian authorities, in their attempt to deny the existence of 'filtration camps' revealed by Amnesty International, did not permit the UN High Commission on Human Rights to visit the camps. On the subhuman conditions in the pre-trial detention centres, which held a million people, Amnesty asserts: "Hundreds of thousands of people awaiting trial continued to be held in grossly overcrowded conditions. Thousands had to sleep in shifts...Tuberculosis and skin diseases were widespread. ...10,000 inmates died each year and more than 100,000 suffered from tuberculosis."

In stark contrast to the Russian record, when the Chechen warriors rounded up the Russian Prisoners of War, they returned them to their mothers, without any precondition. This action of clemency started a new Russian movement called Soldiers' Mothers. On the other hand, the Chechen civilians who fell into Russian hands were let go only after paying a ransom, which their relatives had to raise. Even bodies of the dead had to be purchased for burial.

Lyoma Usmanov, the President of the United States -

Chechen Republic Alliance, Representative of the Chechen Republic to the United States, in his detailed report dated 23 December 1999 States that the Chechens never murdered any humanitarian aid-workers. The Russian undercover agents were involved in this conspiracy. The Russian Federal Secret Service, formerly, the KGB has destroyed the infrastructure and communication system in Chechnya and is actively engaged in anti-Chechen propaganda, portraying them as 'blood-thirsty' people.

The report of Usmanov states that in the immediate aftermath of the Russian invasion, nine out of ten Chechen families did not have enough to eat; 74,000 were left disabled including 19,000 children, 2,000 blind and 1,500 deaf and 12,000 orphaned. Every second newborn infant did not live beyond the first month. Children were born deformed. All the pediatric facilities were destroyed. All four institutions of higher education were destroyed, including state archives and the national museum. The report makes an important point that if Russia considered Chechnya as an integral part of the Russian Republic, then why was not a single Chechen included among the 35,000 Russians sent to the United States for education? Why was Chechnya not classed as one of the 40 regions in need of food assistance from the United States?

10

Banking on the Ghastly Crime of September 11

As a prelude to the scenario of post-September 11, one has to comprehend the perception of the US policymakers on a number of vital global issues. This is based on the notion that world security has to be worked out the American way. Under the Bush Administration's rationale, the Kyoto Accord was unacceptable as it would be detrimental to Corporate America. The ban on illicit exports of small arms and weapons was unacceptable as it would encroach upon the civil rights of the Americans. The formation of a permanent war crimes tribunal was unacceptable as it would restrict the operational decisions on the ground by the American generals and troops. The treaty banning biological weapons was not acceptable either.

The US was not prepared to ratify the UN Convention on the Rights of the Child because it would contravene certain state laws. It could not join the Mine Ban Treaty despite the appeal of the 'International Campaign to Ban Landmines'. It seemed the United States had given itself the power of veto over international accords and agreements.

On his first visit to Europe on 13 June 2001, after having been elected as President of the United States, George W. Bush endeavoured to sell the 'rogue nations' theory, which did not impress his hosts. In the parlance of the American Administration, 'rogue nations' are those countries in the 'Third World', which, despite international economic sanctions either have or are likely to have nuclear capabilities. They are to be feared before they become powerful enough to cause menace to the United States or its allies. The media were grooming American public opinion to the growing threat of terrorism against American life and property. But the statistics available proved otherwise.

Chapter 10 : Banking on the Ghastly Crime of September 11

Quoting the State Department's report, 'Patterns of Global Terrorism 2000', *The New York Times* pointed out that 153 out of 423 incidents were considered 'significant' by the CIA. Only 17 of these were directed against the American interest. The paper wrote that, "...when the threat of terrorism is used to justify everything from building missile defense to violating constitutional rights", it was time to be concerned.[120] The article identified the interest groups who benefited from the myths at the expense of concrete facts.

Charley Reese outlined the main reasons for the Bush Administration's insistence on Intercontinental ballistic missiles. He stated in his analytical article that Bush sought to "dominate the world" without challenge. He warned that this was the "road to endless conflicts" rather than peace.[121]

Former President Jimmy Carter called Bush's Star Wars programme "technologically ridiculous" in his interview in the Columbus *Ledger-Enquirer*. He said that he was "disappointed with almost everything he (Bush) has done."[122]

Nevertheless, the project of 'Sons of Star Wars' (why not 'Daughters of Star Wars'?) was being marketed to the allies, despite the fact that it would have opened avenues for a frantic race in spreading the arsenal.

Jacques Chirac, the President of France, reacted in a pragmatic way on this issue. He expressed his concern that the proposals of the United States could develop into an unbridled missiles-defence race. President Bush got the message on his first visit to Europe. There was a growing feeling among European people and leaders that the proposed missile system was motivated by self-interest only. Even Russia was not impressed.

Demonstrations in the European cities greeted Bush with hostility rather than hospitality. The issue of immediate concern was environmental pollution and global warming, which the United States was adamant to shelve permanently.

Simultaneously with the G8 Summit, the Conference on Climate was taking place in Bonn to ratify the UN Kyoto protocol. The delegates from 178 countries were exhaustively debating the accord. Several hundred scientists and meteorologists believed that

Chapter 10 : Banking on the Ghastly Crime of September 11

the earth is warming up rapidly and that by the end of the century the global temperatures may rise by as much as 42°F. This would almost certainly result in, according to the experts, "crop failures, water shortages, increased diseases and disasters for towns and cities from flooding, landslides and sea storm surges..."[123]

The Conference on Global Warming was focusing on serious issues. After several days' deliberations, which included political manoeuvring, the Conference did reach a compromise agreement. But the odd-man-out was Uncle Sam. The US was simply not interested in the mandatory commitments to reduce greenhouse gases. It was fighting for the rights of its heavy industries to emit gases detrimental to the global climate. Although the US has less than five percent of the world population it is the world's largest emitter of greenhouse gases.

The message that was conveyed from the European cities on Bush's first and second visit was loud and clear. The global environment cannot be sacrificed to the interests of the American corporations. The inhabitants of this planet cannot tolerate uncontrolled emission of poisonous gases into the air.

Angry demonstrations at Gothenburg and Genoa erupted into violence. But they left some food for thought for the leaders of the eight industrial countries. The silent majority and the violent minority wanted the G8 to deal with more pressing international issues, which they felt that the world leaders were brushing aside. The environmentalists wanted a definite commitment from the politicians to make the world a safer place to live in.

The same demands were put forward by the demonstrators when the G8 were meeting in the 2002 and 2003 Summits. The Summit of 2002 was held in solitary confinement in Kananaskis, Alberta in Canada to avoid troublesome protesters. It focused only on three issues – sustaining global growth, combating terrorism and reducing poverty in Africa. The Summit of 2003 was held in Evian-les-Bains in France. Committed protestors arrived in thousands from various parts of the country to express their deep-felt concern that globalization had become a second name for exploitation of the poor nations by the rich ones.

Chapter 10 : Banking on the Ghastly Crime of September 11

The 2001 G8 Summit observed in its final communiqué that over 800 million people remain seriously malnourished, including at least 250 million children. It made commitments to alleviate world poverty and write off some 'Third World' debts, at a time when President Bush was seeking commitment from the world leaders for the next stage in the missiles-defence system. The consensus was not forthcoming. Therefore, a face-saving communiqué had to be worked out with the Russians. Bush had to reassure Putin that the United States and Russia have grown up and have left the Cold War era behind them. They are on a new friendship spree. They would not resort to hostility in future. Therefore, President Putin has yet to understand as Tony Blair has quite understood President Bush's political philosophy on 'rogue nations'.

Bush returned from Europe disappointed. The Pentagon was in the grips of the hawks. They were keen to pursue an aggressive defence strategy. Pearl Harbour was remembered where, on 7 December 1941, 366 Japanese bombers unexpectedly attacked US warships killing 2403 Americans.[124] As a member of the Project for a New American Century, Paul Wolfowitz said as far back as 1998 that it needs a disaster of the scale of Pearl Harbour to awaken American people to the "threat of Arab terrorism"[125].

Several years before the terrible atrocity committed on September 11, the neoconservative radicals had planned their crusading strategy. A tragedy of the scale of September 11, which touched the hearts of many people around the world, naturally warranted an immediate public inquiry of what went so drastically wrong with US security. What happened to the most developed and sophisticated security apparatus in the world? How did the security of the nation become so slack overnight? Who was behind the collaboration with the terrorists? Who benefited politically from the terror attack?

The 900-page declassified final report of congressional investigation was published in late July 2003. It contained new evidence that the CIA and the FBI "knew far more about some of the hijackers' activities than has been revealed".[126] But the report carried many blanked-out pages. It was obvious that the Administration was

Chapter 10 : Banking on the Ghastly Crime of September 11

trying to conceal some revealing evidences of the domestic and foreign involvement in the crime. Despite the insistence of the Saudi government urging the Bush Administration to reveal the contents of the obliterated pages, the Administration was not willing to do so.

As the congressional inquiry was progressing, there were complaints of non-cooperation on the part of the government departments. Joel Skousen writes that the congressional report is very critical of the government's "foreknowledge, failure to respond, and cover-up of suspicious activities..."[127] The President's legal advisors tried to invoke 'executive privilege' to prevent key documents falling into the hands of the investigators for the National Commission on Terror Attacks. The writer says that as reported in *Newsweek,* a committee member was even denied access at Capitol Hill to the transcripts of the meeting.

The victims' representatives are curious to know why the government is denying having shot down one hijacked plane over Pennsylvania despite the overwhelming evidence. They are enquiring, why the fighter inceptors were not allowed to fly after the news of the hijacks was broadcast? Why were the cell phone calls from the hijacked airlines faked? How were the pictures and intelligence information on the night-clubbing, drinking and womanizing activities of the hijackers so readily supplied by the government agencies? How the passports of the hijackers were so rapidly salvaged intact from the ruins of the tower buildings? Why did the list of hijackers include the people who are still alive? Why was there a rush to sell the shares of American airline corporations just prior to September 11? Who were the lucky profiteers and how did they obtain the precise information that the share prices of the airliners were about to sink? These and many other questions of public concern have simply been evaded.

The capitalization of the event of September 11 did not stop at thrusting the nation into two major wars, but in promoting bigotry, and thus violating all the values of freedom and democracy for which the American founding fathers had fought. Peter Beinart, editor of the *New Republic* summarizes the mood. He writes: "The nation is now at war and in such an environment domestic political dissent is immoral."[128]

A very informative expository article by Patrick J. Buchanan explores the Israeli involvement in Bush's National Security Strategy.[129] He exposes many issues, risking the inevitable attempt of being branded 'anti-Semitic'. He quotes Robert Kaiser, who quotes a senior US official in the *Washington Post* (9 February 2003) as saying, "the Likudniks are really in charge now" in the Bush Administration. But he asks, whatever is in Sharon's interest, is it necessarily in America's interest?

The writer asserts that the lined-up war plans against certain nations are bound to jeopardize the US interest with the Muslim world. He condemns the attempts by neoconservatives to 'subordinate' the US interests. September 11 came as a blessing in disguise because the very next day, Bill Bennett suggested to the CNN that war must be declared by the Congress on 'militant Islam'. Not one of a number of countries named by these elements was even remotely implicated in the September 11 tragedy. Four days later, Paul Wolfowitz wanted the US to attack Iraq because it was 'doable', as he put it.

In her excellent exposé on policy study, Phyllis Bennis describes Washington's strategy of pre-emptive strike "to go to war when and where and against whom and for as long as we like..." The pre-war "unilateralism" is followed by post-war "triumphalism". Washington has used the tools of economic aid and trade agreements to bully or bribe the small coalition partners into rallying behind its war on Iraq,[130] she writes.

On 20 September 2001 the neoconservatives urged Bush to annihilate Hizbollah despite the fact that Hizbollah was not at all involved in the September 11 crime. But by banking on human tragedy, they were bent on serving the Zionist agenda. Hizbollah had to be a terrorist organization in the neoconservative dictionary, as, among all the warring parties against Israel, it was the only one that had "humiliated Israel by driving its army out of Lebanon", writes Phyllis Bennis.

Michael Ledeen, the ex-Pentagon officer and a resident scholar at the American Enterprise Institute has even advocated that

Chapter 10 : Banking on the Ghastly Crime of September 11

the US should destabilize Iran, Iraq, Syria, Lebanon and Saudi Arabia. He asserts that their destruction would be, as he put it, "to advance our historic mission". The writer traces how Sharon's pronouncements were being crystallized in the neoconservatives' disastrous strategy for America. In July 2002 Laurent Murawiec had called Saudi Arabia "the kernel of evil...the most dangerous opponent". According to him, the ultimatum to be given to that country was, either you obey or else "we seize your oil fields, and occupy Mecca". No distinction was to be made between the allies and the aliens under the new offensive of the Zion-neoconservatives.

In the aftermath of the Jenin massacre, Bush kept on calling on Sharon to withdraw his forces from the West Bank. He repeated several times in his public statements that he was 'serious' this time. But who eventually gave up, Bush or Sharon? After suffering repeated rebuffs, Bush had to give up, and his staffer at the Center for Security Policy supported the stance adopted by Sharon.

Clauses like 'either for us or against us', 'axis of evil', 'crusade' and 'Sharon man of peace' have to go down in the Guinness Book of World Records. The speechwriters of the dignitaries are paid hefty salaries to select their words and expressions carefully, and this is precisely what they meant when they put words into the mouth of the President that he was to embark on a 'crusade'. This raised the eyebrows of many people in the UK. The hawkish agenda attracted analytical coverage in the BBC TV programme *Panorama* on 18 May 2003.

Christopher Hoskins in the *Financial Times* expresses his concern that it seems "Bush Christian fundamentalists have struck a bizarre alliance with the religious extremists in Israel, whose objectives are to widen their country's territorial ambitions".[131]

Ledeen works closely with Richard Perle, the ex-chairman of the Defence Policy Board. "Richard Perle has been a behind-the-scenes fixture of Washington's neoconservative 'Likkudite' community for more than 20 years." Jim Lobe further writes: "Ledeen's right-wing Italian connections – including alleged ties to the mysterious P-2 Masonic Lodge..." is noteworthy. The Lodge itself had links, as he puts it, to "Italian government, the Mafia, the

Chapter 10 : Banking on the Ghastly Crime of September 11

Vatican and the KGB". When Ledeen returned to Washington in 1981, he was given some very high profile appointments, including, advisor to the Secretary of State, Haig.

Because of their opposition to war on Iraq, Ledeen questioned whether France and Germany were, to quote him, "in league with al-Qaeda and Saddam..."! He even intimated that France and Germany be treated as "strategic enemies". His list of the so-called terror masters comprises "Iran, Iraq, Syria and Saudi Arabia" as the "big four". This naked war-mongering, which he believes should become a permanent feature of US policy, has become a sacrament of neoconservatives. Along with the American Israeli Public Affairs Committee (AIPAC), Ledeen's group, the Coalition for Democracy (COD) is seeking $50 million Congressional approval to promote unrest in Iran. This is an open invitation to terrorism in a foreign country.

Obscene imperialist aims are promulgated on the web pages of the American Enterprise Institute, whose members were referred to by President Bush as some of the "finest brains in our country". Michael Ledeen is a resident scholar at the AEI. Richard Perle is a resident fellow at the AEI, the think-tank that is financed through tax-free donations of unidentified donors. When it makes ridiculous spurious claims, it also musters power to convince itself that its claims are true. The American Enterprise Institute, the Washington Institute and Middle East Forum, writes Brian Whitaker in his highly readable exposé, "promote views from only one end of the political spectrum". The hold of these privately financed organizations is robust on the media empire in America. He writes that "American universities have about 1400" specialists on the Middle East, with about "400-500...experts". Yet he stresses, "their views are rarely sought or heard, either by the media or the government".[132] These institutes do not hide their unequivocal support for and links with Israel. Their advice is valued at the State and Defence Departments in Washington.

Michael A. Ledeen calls in his article for the removal of the Syrian and Iranian regimes.[133] The writer enlists Bin Laden's al-Qaeda as one of the organizations taking instructions from Syria and

Chapter 10 : Banking on the Ghastly Crime of September 11

Iran to fight the US. In their burning ambition to influence US policies, the Zion-neoconservatives do not hesitate to produce a cocktail of polemics and fiction. Ledeen includes Syria and Iran as an "integral part of the terror network that produced September 11..." As the threatening tone of Washington cooled down in August 2003, Sharon came up with a fanciful story that Iran wants to fly a hijacked plane into its own towering buildings in Tel Aviv. This was a desperate attempt to connect Iran with September 11 and to induce the State department in Washington to resume its rhetoric.

Many people around the world do believe, and their theories and arguments are flooded onto the internet, that it was the rivalry between the CIA and the Pentagon that produced September 11. The CIA was demoted after the Cold War and had no covert or overt jobs to do. After September 11, it was once again promoted with a gigantic annual budget worth several billion dollars.

Ledeen presents 'democratization' proposals for Iran. The Administration should install, in his words, "the late shah's son, ...widely admired inside Iran despite his refreshing lack of avidity for power or wealth". This is an insult to basic common sense, which is indeed very uncommon these days in power politics. Do the neoconservatives possess psychic power to know who is widely admired in a country that has no diplomatic or economic or commercial or social or cultural or educational ties with the US?

Ledeen's predictions on Iraq could provide an insight into seventeenth century imperialist conviction. He considers the anti-war coalition as an impediment to Bush's 'instinctively inclined' policies. In his article 'How We Could Lose', he alleges that Crown Prince Abdullah's plan for solving the Palestinian crisis was an attempt to "deflect" America's war against "terror masters". His Iranophobia tilts more towards extremes than Saudiphobia. He accuses the Saudis of financing the network of terror and therefore, calls that "mosques run by the Saudis all over the world" be shut down.

The conjecture on which Ledeen instinctively relies is remarkable. He includes the two private snipers who murdered several people in the Washington area as part of the terror network, in as much as his colleagues had considered the terror caused by

Chapter 10 : Banking on the Ghastly Crime of September 11

McVeigh, the Oklahoma bomber, as the work of 'Islamic fundamentalist'. He warns that the terror Armageddon is bent on destroying the West, whilst the Europeans are busy paraphrasing the UN resolutions, and their foreign ministries preach appeasement.

The Europeans have fortunately grown out of paranoia and do not allow their foreign policies to be dictated by political phobia. To them the New Europe in any case has to be built on the foundation stones laid by the Old Europe.

The Zion-neoconservative masters in the Bush Administration have sought to steer government policies towards weird ideological commitments. Sharon issued instructions that Iran needs to be tackled immediately after Iraq, so it should be. Ledeen portrays Iran as the "really big prize" that can be won at a "bargain price", with no need to fire "a single bullet" or "a single bomb", as he puts it. Only money has to be spent lavishly and the American media have to bombard the Iranians with vigorous propaganda. This could be quite true only if the foreign policy can be orchestrated with Aladdin's lamp. Ledeen keeps on repeating the American holy mission of promoting 'democracy' in Afghanistan and Iraq. He believes that this mission was subdued because of, to use his phrase, "failed personalities" who advised the President to restrain himself. This advice turned America into a "paper tiger". His list of "failed personalities" is all the more interesting.[134] He has very conveniently forgotten that several months after occupying Iraq, the US has totally failed to restore law and order there let alone introduce any democratic institutions in that country.

Michael Rubin who is assigned at the Pentagon, special advisory plans on Iran and Iraq, is marketing a strange idea that ex-crown prince Hassan of Jordan should take over as the king of Iraq.[135] Every fantasy has to be considered viable, provided it has the potential of serving the supreme American interest. This does not mean to say that ex-Crown Prince of Jordan would have known anything about this fantasy.

Ledeen believes that there is an alliance between the Islamic Republic of Iran and the Palestine Liberation Organization with, according to him, "tons of explosives and weapons from Iran headed

Chapter 10 : Banking on the Ghastly Crime of September 11

for Palestinian territory".[136] This is why, according to him, Iran is the enemy of the 'free world'. What about the tons of explosives and weapons headed from the United States to Israel? Under the same token of crippled logic, this should be a blessing for the free world and peace. The views of the extremist pro-Zionist think-tank are synonymous to the views expressed by some ultra-nationalist and racist Arab journalists, who believe that tons of explosives and weapons are exchanged between Iran and Israel. Both views are governed by conjecture and speculation and both are eccentric.

Ledeen expresses the bizarre view that "Iran and the PLO have been cooperating intimately since 1972".[137] A mere casual reference to history would have revealed that in 1972, Iran was under the savage tyrannical reign of the ally of the United States. But as the Shah was terrorizing the entire region under his committed alliance with Israel, his policy was construed as quite pleasant and gratifying for the 'free world'. It was the Shah's Algiers agreement with Saddam, with the full blessing of the US, which unleashed political crimes and massacres on a draconian scale in Iraq.

The guidelines that the think-tank provides to the Pentagon are far-sighted. It was not coincidental that immediately after the Iraq war, the State and the Defence Departments turned the focus of their attention towards Iran. Donald Rumsfeld shocked the world media when he said on 28 May 2003 that the weapons of mass destruction may never be found in Iraq.

The very next day, Paul Wolfowitz, Rumsfeld's deputy told the American magazine *Vanity Fair*: "For bureaucratic reasons we settled on one issue, weapons of mass destruction because it was the one reason everyone could agree on." But why were the defence strategists applying different standards to people of different complexion? Diplomacy was considered a viable option for North Korea who had announced that it would not abandon its nuclear programme. Whereas, military action was the only option for Iraq who had announced that it had abandoned its weapons programme. Wolfowitz was asked to clarify this point at a conference in Singapore and he replied: "The most important difference between North Korea and Iraq is that economically, we just had no choice in

Chapter 10 : Banking on the Ghastly Crime of September 11

Iraq. The country swims on a sea of oil."[138] This means that after all, it was all about oil.

On 28 May 2003, in their brilliant news and analysis coverage, *Channel 4, BBC 2 Newsnight* and *Sky News*, in sharp contrast with the American TV channels' coarse and biased analysis, enquired whether the US and UK intelligence information was unfounded in the first place, claiming that Iraq had weapons of mass destruction. Had the US and UK governments lied and misled the public? Allegations were made in the left-wing quarter of the Labour party that the justification for war was concocted. Rumsfeld might have thought that he could simply pass a statement and walk away, but his about-turn attracted headlines on almost all the main English TV channels. The *Sky News* reporter, quite credibly suggested that there might have been a secret deal between the US and Israel. In return for Sharon's acceptance of the 'road map', the US would have undertaken to address the Israeli concerns over Iran, and hence, a noticeable escalation of war of words against Iran was initiated by the Pentagon.

In his interview with *The Times* before the war, Sharon had already said that after winning the war with Iraq, the next day the world would have to focus on Iran. Therefore, was the Pentagon addressing Sharon's worries by preparing the American public for the forthcoming conflict?

It seemed that etiquette in international diplomacy had gone berserk. For instance, in the meeting on 31 March 2003 of the American Israel Public Affairs Committee (AIPAC), an influential Zionist lobby, top officials in the US government issued threats to the major Muslim countries, Iran and Syria. There was hardly an Arab satellite channel that did not give prominence to this news. The warnings were issued by standing on a Zionist platform. It was not clear whether these officials were representing the US or Israeli interest, in view of the fact that the Administration has time and again claimed that it is a friend of Muslims. Not surprisingly, they got a standing ovation from their Zionist audience, but their speeches added anxiety in the Muslim world as to whether the Administration is to be trusted when it claims that 'the war on terror' is not a war

Chapter 10 : Banking on the Ghastly Crime of September 11

against Muslims and Islam.

Observing the sequential measures that the Bush Administration adopted after September 11, no other than Arabs and Muslims were victimized. But Arabs and Muslims have also become accustomed to what is a habitual procedure in Western politics of victimizing the aggressors and criminalizing the victims. When Israel shoots with live ammunition at close range and kills stone-throwing children, Israel is always the victim and the murdered children and youngsters are 'terrorists'. Such is the crooked logic that has been fed into the minds of the American public. Otherwise, no one would deny the enormous contribution that the American people have made and are making to science and technology, in the promotion of knowledge, in charitable activities, in material progress and development, in the wonderful and fascinating construction of their towns and cities, in space exploration, and in many other humanitarian projects.

The controversial 'anti-terrorism' laws which, many Americans believe, violate the very constitution of the United States by encroaching upon civil liberties, was the brainchild of the American Jewish Congress as far back as 1995. Clinton addressed the World Jewish Congress in New York on 30 April 1995 and according to Edward Said, "pandered to Israel's obsession with Iran..."[139] In that year, although the Oklahoma bombing was the work of homebred terrorists, the American Jewish Congress exploited the already widely prevailing notion that all terrorists were 'Muslims and Arabs'. The AJC advocated banning fundraising for Muslim and Arab organizations as a world-wide fight against terrorism. These dictates of the American Jewish Congress later on became cornerstones in the Bush Administration's priorities. All the signs of "Christian and Jewish extremism were muted" and Muslims were projected as the principal threat.[140]

The Muslim population in the United States is almost seven million. Under the laws of the country, the citizens enjoy certain civil rights. The Constitution of the United States prohibits discrimination on the basis of ethnicity or religion. But what can one make (?) of Dr Daniel Pipes's statement in *The Jerusalem Post* of 22 January 2003,

Chapter 10 : Banking on the Ghastly Crime of September 11

when he said: "There is no escaping the unfortunate fact that Muslim government employees in law enforcement, the military, and the diplomatic corps [in the US] need to be watched for connections to terrorism, as do Muslim chaplains in prisons and the armed forces."[141] For many years, the writings and speeches of Daniel Pipes have become synonymous to Medieval type anti-Islam and anti-Muslim malevolence. Dr Pipes also said: "Muslim visitors and immigrants must undergo additional background checks. Mosques require a scrutiny beyond that applied to churches, synagogues and temples. Muslim schools require increased oversight to ascertain what is being taught to children."[142] Nazi victims could testify that this scenario sounds all too familiar. In many cases, his rhetoric of hatred, with denial of the established facts of history, has defied intellectual responsibility. Paradoxically, the vision of these elements for New America is reminiscent of a Police State with the imposition of Stalinist policies over its Muslim citizens. Yet, they claim that their thinking is in the interest of democracy, freedom and liberty. It is amazing that President George W. Bush deemed it appropriate to nominate Dr Pipes to serve on the United States Institute of Peace in the midst of protest from Interfaith Alliance.

The purpose of the Institute of Peace has been described as "an independent, nonpartisan federal institution created by Congress to promote the preservation, management, and peaceful resolution of international conflicts". When the Senate Committee was convened to consider President Bush's nomination, Senator Edward Kennedy said that the purpose of the US Institute of Peace was promotion of peace and he continued, "I believe that the statements and writings of Dr Daniel Pipes are just the opposite". President Bush had assured and reassured the Muslims that his war was not against Islam. But his advisors have not taken the trouble to familiarize themselves with the strange ideology of the President's nominee.

Addressing the 25th Annual Young America's Foundation National Conservative Student Conference in Washington DC, Dr Pipes rejected the idea of distinguishing between radical terrorists and other Muslims. He said that "there is no history behind such an outlook and nothing that would support such optimism". He further

Chapter 10 : Banking on the Ghastly Crime of September 11

stated that the US should have refrained from supplying food aid to the Afghan civilians, as, "in a time of war, they are the enemy". Likewise, he believed that the US should limit its financial aid to the United Nations Relief and Works Agency (UNRWA) due to its support of "Palestinians remaining in refugee camps".[143] Where are the humanitarian and peaceful gestures in all these suggestions?

In sharp contrast to the views of many American academicians and politicians who protested at the nomination of Dr Pipes, Tashbih Sayeed, the president of the Council for Democracy and Tolerance and editor-in-chief of a California-based newspaper, *Pakistan Today* supported Dr Pipes, notwithstanding the latter's obsession with anything and everything to do with Muslims. Mr Sayeed expressed his own views about the Council of American-Islamic Relations. He said that the aim of CAIR was "waging a war against America in America for their objectives in the Middle East…"[144] Mr Sayeed did not explain though whether the opposition recorded by the Senators and American professors to the nomination of Dr Pipes was also aimed at "waging a war against America in America"?

Mr Sayeed should have studied the campaign that CAIR has undertaken in the last few years for the civil rights of the aggrieved and wrongly treated Muslim citizens of America, including many Pakistanis. If so, he could not have failed to notice that this organization has won the respect of Muslims worldwide, including in today's Pakistan. It needs to be seen whether Mr Sayeed's support for Dr Pipes would affect the latter's views on "brown-skinned people cooking strange foods"[145] who pose a threat to the security of America.

The idea of fighting America in America is a ludicrous thought. The idea of fighting America outside America is equally ridiculous. Professor Niall Ferguson writes that with 750 military bases in "three-quarters of the countries of the world, and 31% of all wealth…" it can only be deduced that the US is an empire. He says that the example of Iraq proves that it is not the job of the armed forces to create law and order. He asserts that the officials who are "in charge of the defence department have grabbed September 11 as

Chapter 10 : Banking on the Ghastly Crime of September 11

a chance to push through the imperial agenda".[146]

Throughout the bombing in Afghanistan, Bush and Blair assured the Muslims that this war was not against Islam, but against international terrorism. Bush visited the Washington mosque and Blair met Muslim leaders at 10 Downing Street, to pacify Muslim public opinion at home and abroad, emphasizing that after all, Muslims are decent people and their religion is peaceful.

With the attention of the world media focused on Afghanistan, Israel decided that this was the best opportunity to unleash its own terror on Palestinian civilians. A record number of shootings and demolition madness was conducted during this period. Israel was confident that its repressive policies would not attract the slightest condemnation in Washington. Despite the grim situation in the Palestinian territories and Afghanistan, Bush sought to reassure the Muslims that they have nothing to fear. He appealed: "I wanted to ensure people that there are common values, even though we may have different ways to worship God."

However, in his backyard, a radical cleric was spoiling the party. The evangelist, Franklin Graham claimed that Islam is a "very evil and wicked religion". He repeated his ill-conceived notion on *NBC Nightly News* (16 November 2001). He said: "The God of Islam is not the same God. He's not the Son of God of the Christian or Judeo-Christian faith. It's a different God, and I believe it is a very evil and wicked religion."[147]

The evangelist was hypocritical in trying to accommodate Jewish faith into the "Son of God" doctrine, when he should have been more aware than anybody else that the Jews do not believe in Jesus as the "Son of God". The Orthodox Jews believe that the blessed Jesus was an "imposter". Billy Graham, Franklin Graham's father is one of the most favourite evangelists of President Bush.

At the crossroads of the bombing on Afghanistan and Israel's high-handed measures, which invited a series of suicide bombings, the Right-wing neoconservatives were trying to make their presence felt. Martin Kramer of the Washington Institute and former director of the Moshe Dayan Centre at Tel Aviv University, who lectures in the United States and Israel, criticized the academicians who showed

Chapter 10 : Banking on the Ghastly Crime of September 11

moderation and a sympathetic attitude towards the study of Islamic politics.

John L. Esposito, a leading American scholar on Islam and the author of the educational and very informative books *Islamic Threat - Myth or Reality?* and *Islam the Straight Path*, commented that these critics are divided into two camps. "One of them believes that all Islamic fundamentalists groups or movements are a threat. The other, represented by myself and several others, would say that you have to distinguish between mainstream Islamic society and extremists, who attack people in their own societies and now in the West."[148]

Quite understandably, Kramer's book *Ivory Towers on Sand* has been published by the Washington Institute for Near East Policy, which has cordial relations with Israel. Esposito continued: "If you look at his own ideological profile and that of his publisher - which are not primarily concerned with what is best for America - it's clear that there is an agenda here, which is to discredit the entire Middle East establishment".[149]

The back garden of President Bush was being filled with Islamophobes, who were putting pressure that Muslims be excluded from debates in connection with national politics. The organizers of World Affair Forum came under this type of pressure and rejected the campaign by the radical fundamentalist American Jewish Committee to exclude Muslim speakers from a public forum to promote intercultural understanding.[150] So much for freedom of speech and democratic values of pressure groups.

Through its arrogant stance, the American Jewish Committee sought to hijack the forum of 'Understanding Islam' for its own ulterior motives. The *Washington Post* quoted a leader from one of the Jewish groups saying: "There is no such thing as peaceful Islam. Islamics cannot fit into an America. (sic) They should be encouraged to leave. They are a fifth column in this country."[151]

In the aftermath of the atrocities of September 11, the Muslim community and religious scholars worldwide, made it absolutely clear, that no person, with any religious conscience could possibly condone indiscriminate killings of innocent civilians. But the Jewish

Chapter 10 : Banking on the Ghastly Crime of September 11

lobby and its right-wing Christian supporters feared that the American defence policy might not remain for long their concubine in the light of the Administration's attempt to seek support for war on terror from the Muslim world. Therefore, they started their smear campaign against Islam and Muslims with renewed ferocity. As a result, Muslims in the United States and Britain were targeted, with physical assaults on their persons and property and arbitrary arrests without trial.

On the other side of the spectrum, intellectual hooligans were embarking upon a campaign of misrepresenting the Islamic faith and its sacred personages. As the war was being won in Afghanistan, the need for respecting the sensitivities of the Arab allies diminished drastically. No voices in official circles were heard any more about Muslims being decent and respectable people. No opinion was expressed any more that Islam was a peaceful religion. After winning the war in Afghanistan, the first diction of betrayal was faced by the Muslim world when the US decided to veto the proposal to send UN observers to the occupied territories to examine and investigate Israeli massacres, which Sharon and his lobby in Washington were intent on concealing.

The question still remains in the minds of many Arabs and Muslims. Are the US policymakers plunging their country into an outright conflict against the Arab and Muslim world under the guise of 'war on terror' by capitalizing on the tragedy of September 11?

11

The Crime of Indiscriminate Killings and Reaction of the Biased Media

JACK Straw, the Foreign Secretary made some revealing disclosures in the *Human Rights Annual Report 2001,* which he presented to the Parliament. It is worth examining some of these points. The Report acknowledged the murder carried out by the Israeli forces of 12-year-old Rami [Mohammad] al-Durra in October 2001 and the killing of 13 unarmed Arab citizens of Israel by Israeli and Border Police. The perplexing question for many Arab-Israeli citizens was: Would Israel have been so liberal in shooting its Jewish citizens in similar circumstances? This explains that equality of citizenry in Israel is a fantasy. The outcome of the three-year inquiry into the shooting of 13 of its own Arab citizens was published in August 2003, absolving the ex-prime minister Ehud Barak and Israeli forces from any responsibility, in line with expectation.

The *Human Rights Report* says, "Israel has long argued that the threats to its security justify measures that violate the human rights of the Palestinians... Palestinian groups justify fatal attacks on Israeli civilians because of the continued occupation of the Palestinian territories" (p. 10). On extrajudicial killing, the report says, the EC and Britain have objected to this practice. The UK has also protested against the illegal practice of detaining the suspects without charge since *Al-Aqsa Intifada* (p. 11). The report mentions torture being used against the detainees. It writes: "In addition to restrictions on movements the IDF has demolished factories, homes, agricultural land and olive groves ..." It remarks that the practice of depriving the Palestinians of their livelihood has escalated the violence. All the points mentioned in Jack Straw's report are as valid today as they were two years ago.

During the war in Afghanistan, Israeli spokesmen used to

155

Chapter 11: The Crime of Indiscriminate Killings and Reaction of the Biased Media

justify to the media their policy of target killings. As long as one Hamas leader could be killed, the murder of civilians and children in the process was considered worthwhile. At the end of the day, it was more than sufficient to claim that any child killing was only an accident.

An Israeli government spokesman took solace from the fact that the Pentagon justified "its killing of dozens of Afghans celebrating a wedding…as an accident…"[152] The US, through its carpet-bombings and strayed bombs in Afghanistan, laid dangerous precedents for the Sharonites. In the massacres that followed in the West Bank, Sharon hailed his assassins and called the killing of one wanted militant a 'great success' despite the fact that several babies, children and women were slaughtered in the process.

A residential apartment building, in a densely populated civilian area in Gaza, was reduced to rubble in the middle of the night. Neither the US government nor the British government issued any meaningful condemnation of this dastardly act. They were confident that, as the massacre of Jenin passed away without any action by the United Nations, the butchery in the heavily populated residential apartment building would not attract any condemnation. They were right. The British government was vigilant enough not to issue a strongly worded statement, just in case it had to be withdrawn later on, with an apology to the Israeli embassy.

On his visit to the Middle East in April 2002, Colin Powell did not respect basic human sensitivity by visiting the refugee camp of Jenin, which had just witnessed a harrowing massacre. Powell was taken instead by his hosts to the Northern Israeli borders. A reporter asked him in the press conference in Jerusalem, why he had not visited the Church of the Nativity, the holiest place in Christianity, which was under siege, and the refugee camp of Jenin, to witness with his own eyes the massacre that had taken place. He evaded the answer with the usual vague gestures. It was quite certain at the time that the US would bar any international investigation and accountability of Sharon for war crimes.

In the face of criticism by the Red Cross and other

Chapter 11: The Crime of Indiscriminate Killings and Reaction of the Biased Media

international humanitarian agencies, the US stood as a spectator to the genocide, which had left the charred bodies of women and children for many days without burial. Jenin was referred to as the ghost town of death, with the intolerable smell of rotting corpses threatening an outbreak of disease.

The reporter of *The Times* of London, wrote from Jenin: "Rarely, in more than a decade of war reporting from Bosnia, Chechnya, Sierra Leone, Kosovo, have I seen such deliberate destruction, such disrespect for human life."[153]

The reporter of *The Independent*, Phil Rees reported monstrous war crimes committed by the Israelis. Even papers such as *The Daily Telegraph*, which traditionally adopts a pro-Israeli line, wrote about devastation on a mass scale. Despite all the shocking evidence of the massacre, the US collaborated in the cover-up.

Channel 4 TV interviewed Jack Straw from Geneva in its main news on 18 April 2002 and asked him whether Britain was doing anything to demand an independent inquiry by the United Nations and other international agencies, and he replied in the affirmative. However, Britain did not pursue its moral responsibility by demanding full inquiry.

Despite the good work that Amnesty International and Human Rights Watch are doing, when Israeli interests are at stake, they adopt a softly-softly approach. From Amnesty International reports, it can be perceived that it holds the Palestinians liable and accountable under 'international statutes', conveniently dismissing the fact that Palestine is not a State and the people are living under occupation. It also forgets that the UN Charters permit the people under occupation to fight the occupiers for self-determination and independence. Alternatively, perhaps Amnesty considers these clauses as abrogated as far as the right of Palestinians to self-determination is concerned.

Paul de Rooij calls the Amnesty reports "shameful" for ignoring serious war crimes against the Palestinians. He cites several examples of downright bias in Amnesty's choice of words. All the adjectives are reserved for the Palestinian violence. That is why

Chapter 11: The Crime of Indiscriminate Killings and Reaction of the Biased Media

perhaps, on the website of the right-wing Jewish organizations, Amnesty is included in the links, simply because its reports do not pose any threat to Israel. It does not distinguish between the oppressors and the oppressed. Nowhere is Amnesty's dubious approach more apparent than concerning the gruesome massacre of Jenin. The UN investigatory team was not allowed by the Israelis to commence its inquiry into the slaughter, and yet, Israel was absolved from any responsibility. Amnesty went ahead in recommending that the Israeli government set up tribunals to try Israeli offenders!

This was equivalent to recommending that the United Nations War Crimes Tribunal appoint Milosevic as its chairman, or recommending that His Holiness the Pope appoint the child molesters and paedophile priests as the heads of Child Care Homes.

Paul de Rooij's excellent paper posted on the web highlights the shortcomings of Amnesty International that often draws equivalents between the torturous sufferings of the entire Palestinian community and those of the Israelis. He writes that it is the Israelis and not the Palestinians who are the occupation force. It is Palestinians and not the Israelis whose children are suffering from malnutrition. At least, as far as the rights of the innocent children are concerned, one would have expected Amnesty to be fair and even handed. It is the Palestinian civilians and not the Israeli civilians who face the daily ordeal of closures, curfews and blockades of medical facilities and beatings.

Rooij illustrates through several examples the disproportionate attitude of Amnesty. On 23 June 2002, Israel dropped a one-ton bomb on a densely populated area of Gaza. This was a crime against humanity that deliberately targeted the civilians sleeping peacefully in their flats. Nevertheless, Amnesty equated the crime with the need for the Palestinian Authority to abide by 'international human rights standards'. It seemed that Amnesty was quite satisfied with Israel's adherence to these standards. Amnesty was charitable in that it actually bothered to comment on this aerial attack after having ignored 42 similar aerial bombardments.

Rooij gives another example of Israeli missile attacks on

crowded streets and a hospital in Khan Yunis on 7 October 2002. Amnesty International ignored altogether the killing of 14 civilians and the wounding of 80 others. However, if similar casualties had occurred on the Israeli side by the suicide bombers, the Israelis would have portrayed Amnesty as an outcast if it had chosen to maintain silence. Similar casualties did occur on 21 October 2002 in the middle of a group of Israeli army personnel, and not civilians. Amnesty was quick to issue condemnation.[154]

If the civilized world can let war crimes on such a gigantic scale as that observed in Jenin go unpunished, it means that the international justice system will go on being held hostage for political motives. People would lose whatever little confidence they have in international law. Every year, billions of dollars' worth of American military supplies are pumped into Israel. This military aid has been the main factor for the total rejection of all peace accords with the Palestinians by successive Israeli governments. This rejection reached its zenith since Sharon was crowned on the throne of the Likud government. Ever since he was a soldier in the army, he believed only in the use of force. The US with the American taxpayers' money has facilitated Sharon's intransigence and ambition for a 'greater Israel'.

But it is a great consolation that there are peace-loving men and women of conscience in the West. The youth arm of Sweden's ruling party filed an official complaint against Sharon for crimes against humanity.[155] The complaint by the SSU youths of the Social Democratic Party also included the Israeli government, military commanders and soldiers. "The Palestinians have no possibility to take legal action against crimes committed by Israel in the occupied areas, and therefore we must help them…" said the SSU chairman Mikael Damberg.[156] If a resolution was tabled at the United Nations condemning Israeli actions, the US either opposed or vetoed the resolution outright. Thus, terror has continued without abatement.

Palestinian civilians have faced humiliation every moment of their lives in subhuman conditions in the refugee camps. The youths are left with no education and no work. When Cherie Blair, the wife

Chapter 11: The Crime of Indiscriminate Killings and Reaction of the Biased Media

of the Prime Minister had the courage to say this in public, she was pressurized to withdraw her statement and apologize for speaking the truth.

Bush considers all the repressive measures taken by Sharon, his 'man of peace', as necessary for the sake of peace. The world community stands at the crossroads of either acknowledging that Israel's status is above international law and exempt from humanitarian standards, or face blackmail. The Administration can pull the plug and stop contributing to the funds of the United Nations.

Following the Gaza massacre, the White House spokesman said in the name of the President that the attack was 'heavy-handed'. The Israeli government official could not agree more. Of course, it was heavy-handed, he said. Thank goodness that the White House had shown a lenient way of appreciating the sensitivity of the situation, in the wake of the approaching mid-term congressional elections. The White House also issued a reassuring statement: "The President has been and will continue to be the first to defend Israel."[157] Hence, the Republicans won the mid-term elections.

In stark contrast with this situation, when Israel attempted to assassinate the Hamas leader Abdul Aziz Al-Rantisi in Gaza on 10 June 2003, killing and wounding several innocent bystanders, the personal standing of President Bush was at stake. He had taken a gamble on starting the peace process, which was on the verge of collapse. Therefore, the tone of condemnation was drastically different. Bush said that he did not believe that the assassination policy would help the Israeli security. The next day, Hamas retaliated with a suicide bombing in Jerusalem and within hours Israel retaliated by attacking with helicopters in Gaza. Again, innocent bystanders were killed and injured, ten of them children. Colin Powell and Kofi Annan appeared on 11 June on a common platform and issued strongly worded condemnation against suicide bombing in Jerusalem. The officials in Washington did not have the courtesy to utter a single word of condemnation against the killing of Palestinian civilians, children and bystanders. If they were solemnly

Chapter 11: The Crime of Indiscriminate Killings
and Reaction of the Biased Media

interested in putting an end to this lunacy, they should not have treated the deaths of Palestinian civilians as of lesser importance. Charley Reese writes: "If there is such a thing as evolution, it ain't working, at least as far as the human brain is concerned".[158]

In connection to the missile attack on the Hamas leader, Bush said: "I am troubled by the recent Israeli helicopter gunship attacks". The estranged Democrats in the Congress saw in Bush's statement an opportunity to score some points with the pro-Israeli voters. Thirty-four Democrats signed a protest objecting to the use of the word 'troubled'. They said that they were "deeply dismayed" at Bush's "criticism of Israel"![159]

Israeli officials started to draw a flimsy distinction between civilian deaths on both sides. They said that their action was justified as they had targeted the militants. It did not matter that the majority who were killed were non-militants and passers-by. When a reckless military action is carried out in a heavily congested civilian area, where the civilian casualties can be envisaged with certitude, this is equivalent to deliberately targeting civilians. The rationale applicable to the Palestinian groups is equally applicable to the Israelis. Any distinction is nothing but cunningness and is tantamount to misleading the public.

Following the assassination attempt on the life of the Hamas leader, two British MPs, Oona King and Jenny Tonge, travelling with Christian Aid in Gaza, filed a report describing the torments of life in Gaza for the natives. Ms King, herself Jewish, wrote that more than one million Palestinians are squeezed in a land "smaller than the Isle of Wight". More than 75 percent earn "less than £1.30 a day". On the other side of the spectrum, "5000 Israeli settlers occupy one-third of the land". Sometimes the Palestinians have to put up with the humiliation of waiting for days at the Israeli checkpoints to get basic services, such as, medical care. In some areas, unemployment runs up to 80 percent. Israel even robs the occupied territories of 80 percent of their water supply. Oona King concludes that from what she witnessed, she has no choice but to boycott Israeli products.[160]

Those Arab officials who have humbly surrendered to the

Chapter 11: The Crime of Indiscriminate Killings and Reaction of the Biased Media

will of Sharon, have volumes of lessons to learn from this courageous Jewish British MP, who, not only could see but also feel the pain of the Palestinian Arabs on their own land. There is a great difference between seeing and feeling. Though the writer stressed that Bush should put pressure on Sharon to avert humanitarian disaster, Palestinian rights have long been buried and dehumanized. Even when Bush talks about an independent Palestinian State, he never means a State that enjoys sovereignty over its land, air and water. That sort of privilege he would like Sharon to retain over the Palestinian territories.

Charley Reese discloses a bitter truth which has not been perceived by the American people and which has been categorically ignored by the biased media. He writes: "...It's not fair to call Palestinians terrorists. It is not they who have used tanks, advanced war planes and helicopter gunships against civilians; it is not they who use death squads...; it is not they who imposed collective punishments." Then he draws a sharp contrast between the living conditions of the Palestinians and the Jewish settlers. The latter enjoy "plush lawns, gardens and even a swimming pool" whereas down the hill, the Palestinians have to fetch water from pumps for cooking and washing. He concludes: "...I'm sorry our government is an accessory to war crimes and is such a world-class hypocrite. So long as we ignore the terrible plight of the Palestinians, no American should open his or her mouth about human rights, the rule of law or democracy. ..."[161]

The eye-witness report of Joe Smith posted on the website[162] describes the murder of Rachel Corrie, the American peace activist. She was crushed under an Israeli bulldozer as she tried to save a Palestinian child. It was established by her colleagues that the driver was clearly able to see her approaching. Later, Israel claimed that it was an accident. If it had been an accident, then when the friends of Corrie appealed for help from soldiers in the tank that arrived on the scene, the soldiers should have expressed some remorse and should have been prepared to assist. Instead, they simply walked away, as reported by the eye-witnesses.

Chapter 11: The Crime of Indiscriminate Killings and Reaction of the Biased Media

American peace activists have the interest of the oppressed people at heart, and provide an exemplary, but very embarrassing model for the Arab governments. Over 40 University campuses in the United States pursued their endeavour, in the words of Junaid Alam, to "force American universities to dissociate itself (sic) from companies conducting business with Israel". Norman Finkelstein, a political science professor at DePaul University and the son of a holocaust survivor writes: "If Israelis don't want to stand accused of being Nazis they should simply stop acting like Nazis."[163]

On 25 July 2002, the office of Attorney Stanley L. Cohen in New York issued a press release in connection with the court case that was filed in the United States District Court in Washington, DC on behalf of a group of Palestinian Americans. It said that the case would include a number of children who were killed and others who were injured during Israel's bombing of a civilian neighbourhood in Gaza. The defendants would include "the arms manufacturer of the F-16 jet used in the attack". Cohen challenged Israel's assertion that the operation was either a mistake or isolated. He described the bombing as an "offense to all international law and standards of decency". He stated that the attack was but another deplorable example of Israel's long-standing policy of collective punishment in which it targets all Palestinians for the deeds of a few.

In the lawsuit, the plaintiffs include Palestinian Americans who have been killed, injured, and tortured; and those who were denied medical treatment and whose businesses and homes were destroyed and whose lands were illegally confiscated. There are some three dozen defendants who include Prime Minister Sharon, President Bush and Secretary of State Powell, several arms manufacturers in the United States and a number of US based churches and synagogues that have supported settlements in the West Bank. The plaintiffs seek damages and injunctive relief for genocide, crimes against humanity, war crimes and racketeering, ranging from the massacre at Sabra and Shatila in Lebanon, to the current *Intifada*.

In response to Mr Cohen's argument that the plaintiffs had a well-founded fear of retaliation at the hands of the Israeli Defence

Chapter 11: The Crime of Indiscriminate Killings and Reaction of the Biased Media

Force if their identities were revealed, the Court in the US ruled that they could proceed with the lawsuit using pseudonyms instead of real names.[164]

In an impressive article, Shlomi Segall describes his experience as a teenage conscript in an occupying army.[165] He states that the Israeli "slave market" was the only avenue open for the Palestinian fathers to feed their children. Being a member of the 'Courage to Refuse' movement, he had vowed with his others colleagues, "not to serve...beyond the 1967 line". He believes that "Sharon and his cronies" are continuing their "colonial war". The writer's touchy description of Sharon's provocation can provide food for thought for those US politicians who care to listen and decide, not from their hearts but from their minds. He further describes how Sharon has embarked on, in his words, a "second Nakba" by categorically destroying the Palestinian identity and infrastructure.

Effectively, Sharon has turned Israel into a Police State by silencing the University lecturers with the threat of sacking and jailing of dissidents. The supporters of 'Courage to Refuse' are boycotted. Mr Segall then enlists several human catastrophes that can be credited to Sharon and his fellow generals who do not portray "basic values", as he put it.

The Bush Administration bought time on behalf of the Israeli government by insisting that reforms in the 'corrupt' Palestinian Authority should precede any peace talks. Winning support from the Arab world for war against Iraq was becoming a major issue. Therefore, before and during the war, publicity was given to the 'road map'. After the appointment of Mahmood Abbas 'Abu Mazen', as the new Palestinian Prime Minister, and after adopting the delaying tactics, the 'road map' that was supposed to be a panacea was finally handed over to the concerned parties. The government of Abu Mazen was destined to fall even before the peace talks started.

Michael Hoffman writes: "The diabolically clever Bush/Sharon 'Road Map' serves to enhance the public relations image of the Israeli state, and blacken the image of its victims. ...This is the big picture which the infantilized American people do

Chapter 11: The Crime of Indiscriminate Killings and Reaction of the Biased Media

not grasp and which the American media will not publish or broadcast."[166]

The insistence of the US that the Palestinian Authority must reform itself before any peace talks was not based on any sensible premise. In the last three years for instance, corporate crime in America has rocked the world stock markets. Investors have been defrauded in broad daylight and have lost their lifetime investments in pension funds, under the very nose of the legislators and regulators. Does this mean that until corruption in the American multinational corporations was eradicated, the stock markets should not have been allowed to function? Corporate crime may never cease. Similarly, corruption in the Palestinian Authority may never end completely. As one cannot justify punishing law-abiding investors on the market, so one cannot justify punishing the innocent masses for the misdeeds of a handful of people. The US enjoys staunch relationships with many unrepresentative and non-democratic governments. Under the same token of logic, the US should have stopped having any dealings with these governments until they had enacted democratic reforms.

The West has used the peace process to advance its own purpose. In order to appease public opinion in the Arab world against the war on Iraq, Tony Blair took the initiative of calling an international peace conference in London. The conference was boycotted by Israel. But the initial enthusiasm also fizzled out after the outcome of the war on Iraq. Priorities suddenly changed. The Public Relations exercise directed at the Arab world was muted until the US decided to start the initiative on its own terms.

As reported in *The Muslim News* on 20 May 2003, a group of MPs from all parties criticized the British government for supplying arms and F16 components to Israel via the US, being aware that these will be used in the occupied territories. The MPs said that this "undermines the government's policy".

On publication of the 'road map', the US declared that this was non-negotiable. When Israel insisted that it had reservations, Washington changed its mind and assured Israel that its reservations

Chapter 11: The Crime of Indiscriminate Killings and Reaction of the Biased Media

would be taken into consideration. This means that it was non-negotiable only for the Palestinians. The 'road map' placed the entire onus on the Palestinian Prime Minister to stop the violence. But it did not ask Sharon to put a stop immediately to his own violence. Sharon offered some window-dressings. He ordered illegal settlements to be dismantled. The next day his troops razed the tents and caravans from the sites. The media hailed these measures as a major breakthrough. Sharon's extremists wailed that he had sold out Israel's birthrights.

All these are fabricated attempts to run away from reality, as a result of which, innocent civilians on both sides of the divide have been indiscriminately killed. Had the Israeli leaders willed it, peace could just have been round the corner a long time ago. The world-renowned thinkers and philosophers have not opined on this matter in vain.

In Appendix I of his book *Peace in the Holy Land,* John Glubb quotes a long memorandum, dated 31 January 1970, issued by Bertrand Russell, a few hours before his death. The last paragraph of that historic memo reads: "All who want to see an end to bloodshed in the Middle East must ensure that any settlement does not contain the seeds of future conflict. Justice requires that the first step towards a settlement must be an Israeli withdrawal from all the territories occupied in June 1967. A new world campaign is needed to help bring justice to the long-suffering people of the Middle East." [167]

In Appendix II, John Glubb quotes a three-page article from *The Times* of London of 5 February 1971, under the title, 'America's very special relationship with Israel', by a high-profile US official. He had spent 26 years in the United States Foreign Service. He makes very important points on the political relationship between the US and the Zionist State. He writes: "Unique...is Israel's almost total immunity from criticism in the United State. ..." He quotes James Reston of the *New York Times,* who said that any criticism of Israel was bound to be branded as anti-Semitism.[168]

The US official continues: "Only history can provide the total explanation for this very special American - Israeli relationship. It

Chapter 11: The Crime of Indiscriminate Killings and Reaction of the Biased Media

has now reached a point where Israel's security and welfare is considered vital to American welfare..." to an extent that the United States can trigger off the 'Third World War' if Israel's survival was threatened, the article says.[169] This article was written before Israel shocked the world with the size of its nuclear arsenal, which is capable of destroying the world twice over. But Washington has always considered Israel's weapons of mass destruction as a blessing to world peace. Since the article was written in 1971, the US has demonstrated on many occasions that it considers Israel's violations of human rights and snubbing of UN resolutions beyond criticism.

Not unsurprisingly, in 1971, Sharon complained that he had not been able to persuade Golda Meir's ministers to accept his plan for total elimination of the refugee camps.(!) The cabinet ministers however, 'approved wholeheartedly' his proposals for the establishment of Jewish settlements.[170] Many Palestinians believe that Sharon would leave no stone unturned to thwart any 'road map' in order to fulfil his ambition and vision for continuing with the settlements. Indeed, Sharon's lack of will to abide by the American 'road map' claimed its casualty with the resignation of Abu Mazen.

The biased media, more often than not, have not been part of the solution but part of the problem. Even on humanitarian issues such as the use of civilians as pawns in the game of violence, the media have played an unethical role. No person in his right state of mind can applaud the killing of civilians and children. But when the American TV channels report the deaths of Israeli children, they warn their viewers that they may find the scenes disturbing. When Palestinian infants and babies are killed with Israeli bullets, the news goes unreported. Such a discriminatory approach of giving importance to selected human lives, strikes at the roots of the ethical responsibility of the media. Of course, the stereotypes have to satisfy the specified ideas of the media barons, irrespective of what the reality may be.

Charley Reese comments: "About 10 or 12 mega-conglomerates control about 75 percent communications in the United States..." There is less competition in the printing industry as compared to the major developed countries. In the US, with a population of 268 million, there were in 2001, 1480 daily newspapers.[171] These were under the ownership and patronage of a handful of conglomerates. Therefore, an employee on the editorial or reporting staff has to pay political allegiance to the owners, and be tuned to their voice, otherwise, face a backlash.

During the second *intifada* there have been times when for a long period of six to eight weeks no suicide bombing took place. When it was resumed, the rumbling and roaring voices in the media splashed headline news, telling the viewers that with resumed suicide bombing a 'lull' of eight weeks is broken. A lull for whom? The Palestinians never noticed any lull in their daily life. Every single day, the Israelis continued with their terror. So long as no Israeli was being killed, the killing of Arabs was not worth a mention in the US media.

Michael Palumbo writes that in the United States the history books, magazine and newspaper articles about the expulsion of the Palestinians in 1948 only present a one-sided Israeli version of events. No reputable publishing house dares to publish in his words, "honest history" and a balanced account of the forced eviction of the Palestinians from their homes, "...since such a book would quickly be forced out of circulation by the powerful Zionist lobby". He considers "double standards" in America and to a lesser extent, Britain, to be responsible for promoting books on Arab 'terrorism' and labeling books written on Zionist atrocities as 'anti-Semitic'[172]

For many years the Zionists claimed that the Arabs were planning to drive the Jews into the sea at a time when they themselves were driving the Arab natives into the desert. Only the American media were impressed by such baseless propaganda.

In his highly readable book, *The Palestinian Catastrophe: The 1948 Expulsion of a People from their Homeland,* Michael Palumbo writes that even the memoirs of military personnel and the state archives in Israel are subjected to censorship. As Netiva Ben Yehuda said: "This country is filled with stories that won't be told".[173] The example of Hollywood movie *Exodus,* is cited, which

Chapter 11: The Crime of Indiscriminate Killings and Reaction of the Biased Media

carried distortions of history. Palumbo concludes: "It is of course unthinkable that Hollywood could ever produce an honest film about 1948".[174] He gives an example of how the Zionists engineered cancellation of a documentary on American TV in several cities in 1986, just because it carried eye-witness accounts of the Deir Yassin and Dawayma massacres.[175]

David McDowall describes the extent of prejudice in Western public opinion. He writes that the "...Palestinian struggle became synonymous with terrorism. Only a tiny minority who knew the story of Palestine recalled that Israelis were...proficient in the execution of atrocities."[176]

A disabled American Jew was killed by the hijackers of *Achille Lauro* in 1985. He adds: "One American was moved to write an opera, *Klinghoffer*. No one in the West felt sufficiently moved to create a similar artistic work to commemorate the 14,000 or more civilians slain by Israel when it had invaded Lebanon..."[177]

In its all-out war in Lebanon, Israel bombarded American-owned refineries, causing power cuts. The American media's dual loyalty was immediately unveiled. Although the raids were reported, the prominent newspapers in New York did not mention at all that the refineries were American-owned.

On a number of occasions, full-fledged censorship of news and views has been practised in the Zionist-controlled media in the United States. Exaggerated commentaries, one-sided views, blackout of news of the atrocious living conditions of the Palestinians in the occupied territories, are not uncommon.

Incidents against Israel are sensationalized to give an impression that it is the Palestinians who are occupying Israeli territories. In comparison, one has to appreciate the freedom of press and high standards of journalism in Britain and the level of criticism directed at the government officials. If the same level of criticism was directed by the American media at the US government officials, they would have been branded as unpatriotic. There is a generation gap between British and American journalism.

On the bigotry and bias of the media, Edward Said has posted

Chapter 11: The Crime of Indiscriminate Killings and Reaction of the Biased Media

on the web a very informative article.[178] The article exposes the hypocrisy of the system which easily succumbs to pressure through donations and other manipulations.

On his visit to South Lebanon, Edward Said visited Khiam prison, which was built by the Israelis in 1987, in which he writes, "8000 people were tortured and detained in dreadful bestial conditions." He reflects upon the rationale of the Zionists which is that, though the author was born in Jerusalem, he has no right of return, whereas Jews born anywhere in the world have the right of return and the right of settlement. He explains to what extent the Zionist propaganda machinery distorts the truth, misleads international opinion and imposes restrictions on freedom of thought and expression, with the full support of the American media. The article informs of the vendetta Dr Said faced against his own person and position as university professor, with the purpose of silencing his efforts for a lasting just peace and co-existence and an end to occupation. Needless to say, this was a bitter pill for the occupation forces to swallow.

It would of course be irresponsible to claim that the Arab and Muslim media are free from any prejudice or one-sided reporting.

Certain journalists are little concerned about the need for harmony in their reporting standards. They are quite prepared to defend vehemently their political preconceptions, even if that means self-contradiction. The complacency of the garrulous reporters, motivated by blind nationalistic fervour bordering on racism, tends to rely on unsubstantiated reports originating from unreliable espionage sources. Though these reports contravene every bit of evidence in the real world, the reporters make sensational capital out of accusing in particular, Iran, for dealing with Israel. If this were a condemnable act, then they should have had the minimum honesty to investigate their own governments' co-operation, friendship, commercial and economic ties, and surrender to the will of Israel, in exchange for American aid.

In most, if not all the Arab countries, government control over the media does not allow any criticism against government policies. In such an environment, the emergence of *Al-Jazeerah* TV network was a major breakthrough. For the first time, the Arab world was able to witness open debates and discussions, balanced news and views from both sides of the divide and intellectual discourses, with a knack for detailed analysis. The professional approach of the moderators, allowing the expression of opposing opinions on the issues under debate, patches the gap that was lacking in the Arab media. These missing paradigms were filled by *Al-Jazeerah*. It would however be naïve to say that *Al-Jazeerah* is unbiased and does not take sides.

The secret information on Saddam's devilish regime, which has featured in the documentaries and political commentaries, was available to the Arab media long before his disgraceful fall from power. But so long as he was on the throne, the savagery of his rule and that of his aides did not attract fair coverage. The Arab world stood united in Saddam's aggressive war against Iran. The oil-rich countries in the region, supported his ambition politically, financially, militarily and even by twisting and using religion as a scapegoat to justify his aggression. Delegations upon delegations of clerics, specializing in spreading mischief, arrived in Baghdad to congratulate the tyrant for having been honoured to fight 'jihad' against Iran. The US-cum-Israeli intelligence was also playing its role.

The US was humiliated with the loss of the Shah, its agent and policeman in the region. It also suffered the hostage crisis which was a poisonous pill to swallow. Israel had destroyed the nuclear reactor in Iraq but wanted the Iran - Iraq war to continue for 'as long as it takes'. The Arab world too was sapping its energy and wealth in the stubborn war which cost two million lives. Knowing the nature of this dangerous game, anybody could have foreseen that the serpent would eventually turn against its nurturers, and this is how Saddam displayed his true nature. Within three years, he invaded Kuwait and attacked Saudi Arabia with missiles.

When Saddam extended his aggression against Kuwait and Saudi Arabia, the clerics did not talk any more about 'jihad'. Instead,

Chapter 11: The Crime of Indiscriminate Killings and Reaction of the Biased Media

they changed their tone and colour. Such contradictions are rampant in Muslim society. Before advocating 'jihad' against others, these officially sponsored clerics should have started the struggle with themselves. Had they reformed their own thinking and fought 'jihad' with their inner 'selves', they would not have landed up in a menacing situation.

These types of clerics have always to be distinguished from honest, sincere and devoted ones who perform their duties faithfully in the most trying circumstances. In the political world, those who cannot impress the public with pomp, glory, deception and intrigues, are not considered much of a success. Unfortunately, the same criterion is being conspicuously applied even in the religious matters by some people. As a result, a whole class of court-clerics has developed over the centuries, who, whilst speaking in the name of religion, are in fact, spokesmen of their peers.

At times, the opportunist journalists and reporters come up with grotesque stories to fuel the fire of war of words. Yellow journalism and sensationalism exploits both the political and religious environment. It seeks to turn the victims into offenders and vice versa.

In the modern wars and hostilities, each party to the conflict strives to use a powerful medium of propaganda to win public opinion. As the Anglo-American war on Iraq has abundantly illustrated, false information could be projected in a tactical manner in the media, and the public is led to believe that it is true.

Taking the example of the American hostages in the early eighties, as the scandal that came to be known as 'Irangate' unfolded, it was disclosed that there had been a secret deal between the Reagan Administration and Iran for supplies of arms in exchange for the hostages.[179] But the matter was totally distorted for public consumption and the public has never been told the truth.

Iran was a sworn enemy of the US and Israel. The intelligence community in both countries had a profound interest in manipulating the issue of arms-for-hostages to alienate Iran from the Arab and Muslim world. At that time, Saddam was the self-

Chapter 11: The Crime of Indiscriminate Killings and Reaction of the Biased Media

appointed pioneer and pillar of Arab Nationalism. The person who himself was bankrupt of any dignity, spoke in the parlance of Arab dignity. There were people around him who were prepared to lend him their ears. The Israeli connection was introduced although, for all intents and purposes, the deal was with the Reagan Administration. An Israeli spy who was an Iraqi Jew[180] even approached Robert Maxwell, who himself had secret Mossad connections,[181] offering to sell his story on 'Irangate' for $750,000 payment in advance.[182]

The same Israeli agent, allegedly involved in the 'Irangate' arms deal, claimed that he was appointed as, to quote the author, "Number Three at Mossad...later he said he had been promoted to Number Two and finally, after several meetings with Prime Minister Yitzhak Shamir he said he was then Head of Mossad." Nicholas Davies, the author of the book *The Unknown Maxwell,* writes that this secret agent claimed that he was "directly responsible" to Shamir in his capacity as "Special Foreign Adviser". The author concludes: "I just didn't believe him".[183]

Earlier he had taken the author to meet the alleged arms dealers involved in 'Irangate'. Two dealers were Austrians, one was an American, and one was a Pole. All agreed that they wanted to supply arms to Iran and be "paid by the American government". However, they were all unanimous that "they had never sold any arms to anyone anywhere".[184] This is a classic example of how the media could manoeuvre the situation to mislead the public opinion.

These well-documented facts speak for themselves. Yet, by reviving the old nationalistic antagonism, a reporter of *Al-Jazeerah* referred, as recently as 14 June 2003, to the Iran - Israeli arms deals during the 'Irangate' scandal, as if it was Gospel truth. To be fair to *Al-Jazeerah,* when during a separate debate, an Egyptian reporter made lots of noises about Iran's 'good relations' with Israel, the moderator snubbed him saying: "You do not expect anybody to believe that, do you?"

Presenting facts as they are is an ethical responsibility of good journalism. However, there are deficiencies and constraints

Chapter 11: The Crime of Indiscriminate Killings and Reaction of the Biased Media

faced by the independent TV groups. *Al-Jazeerah* is Qatar based, and is most probably financed by the Qatar government. Therefore, it would never trespass into a prohibited area of commissioning its correspondent reports on the cordial relations that Qatar enjoys with Israel. It would never attempt in any of its programmes to discuss the military and logistic facilities kept at the disposal of the Americans by the Qatar government for attacking neighbouring Iraq. It would never inquire how many Iraqi civilians were killed and maimed for life as a direct consequence of the American sorties flown from Qatar.

Notwithstanding these reservations, Qatar has to be commended and given credit for housing a superb TV network such as *Al-Jazeerah*, that has definitely broken the iceberg of bigotry. It has opened up a world of opportunity for the Arabs towards freedom of expression and speech. Sometimes, its coverage of Middle Eastern events has even clashed with the champions of 'freedom and democracy', who, paradoxically sought to restrict its activities. Its website was hacked by the intellectual terrorists. Its reporter was even evicted from the New York Stock Exchange in revenge for televising the American prisoners of war. But when the American media showed the Iraqi prisoners of war, this was construed to be in the interest of 'freedom of expression'. *Al-Jazeerah, Al-Arabiya, ANN, Al-Alam* and a few other independent satellite channels succeeded where the government-controlled media had badly failed. It must be recognized that any shortcomings at this rudimentary stage, are not the end of the world.

On the other side of the spectrum, despite their development, the Western media have not been able to free themselves from bias against the Muslim community. On many occasions, Islamic organizations the world over, have clarified that Islamic teachings are absolutely against indiscriminate killings of civilians and children, for whatever purpose. Harm inflicted on innocent human lives is totally prohibited in Islam and there is no compromise on this issue simply because it is very widely documented in the Islamic sources. The rules of warfare laid down in Islamic legislation are

Chapter 11: The Crime of Indiscriminate Killings and Reaction of the Biased Media

preserved in history. But the Western media, ever so ready to indulge in mudslinging and innuendo, continue using such generalized terms as 'Islamic terrorists', 'Islamic extremists', and 'Islamic fundamentalists', with an emphasis on *Islam*.

The Palestinians faced constant aggression against their life, property, human rights, honour and dignity, and yet, in the American media, it was always the Palestinians who were 'terrorists', 'extremists', 'radicals' and what not? The Jews even issued threats that for every Jew killed they would kill a thousand Arabs.[185] Was this to be construed as a gesture of goodwill?

When Christians indulge in acts of terrorism against each other in Northern Ireland, Rwanda, the Democratic Republic of Congo, Sierra Leone, Liberia and many other places, they are never referred as 'Christian terrorists'. When gangs of ruffians among the Hindus slaughtered helpless members of the Sikh community in India in the aftermath of the assassination of Mrs Indira Gandhi, and when they burnt the Muslims alive in the Gujarat riots, the media did not embark upon a blanket accusation by calling them 'Hindu terrorists'. When successive Israeli governments declare their unholy wars by using military muscle against unarmed civilians, the media never use insulting words by calling them 'Jewish terrorists'.

The irony of the situation is that as Muslims are branded 'terrorists', some countries forget their own squalid record. For instance, the Russian leadership started branding all the Chechens as 'Islamic terrorists'. Despite its own appalling human rights records against the minorities, the Russian regime was now entering into an alliance with the US on what it called, combating 'Islamic militancy' and 'war against terrorism'. If the deprived minorities dare demand justice and civil rights, they are subjected to contempt. The resources of the country are wasted in preserving corrupt bureaucracies rather than promoting equal opportunity and equitable distribution of wealth. The national aspirations of the suppressed minorities are thwarted by considering them as aliens in their own land, as is happening with the Chechens.

It is high time that in light of the realities of twenty-first-

Chapter 11: The Crime of Indiscriminate Killings and Reaction of the Biased Media

century politics, 'terrorism' is redefined. The FBI's own definition does not provide a viable yardstick but leaves several loopholes. It defines terrorism as, "the unlawful use of force or violence against persons or property to intimidate or coerce a government, the civilian population, or any segment thereof, in furtherance of political or social objectives". What happens if governments themselves use unlawful force or violence against persons or property of civilians?

Conclusion

IN modern power politics, small and defenceless states are vulnerable to the expansionist ambitions of the powerful nations. Although the world is divided into two camps, the developed and developing world, the perceptive reality is different. There are developed, developing, under-developed and undeveloped countries. The developed world has taken the role of godfather of the other three. If regional wars of the past century, and recently, of Afghanistan, Iraq and Palestine are of any guidance, then the gluttony of the powerful nations is visible in their endeavour to win other people into their own camp of influence.

We are told that the Bush Administration has proofs that Iran is developing weapons of mass destruction. One can fairly predict what these proofs might be. They could be the intercepted recordings of conversation between officials, the type of evidence that Colin Powell presented to the United Nations in relation to Iraq, and was only able to convince himself. In this case, the US need not go to the UN with intelligence recordings. As Israel is pressing for action against Iran, the hawks in Washington have issued public statements saying that the US reserves the right to take military action. On their websites, they audaciously advocate military adventurism against Iran and even against Saudi Arabia.

North Korea on the other hand, is not an oil-producing country. So Washington's approach to deal with its extensive nuclear development programme is orientated towards diplomacy. Washington has ruled out any military action against that country because there is a strong presence of 36,000 US army personnel next door in South Korea. Any aggression may endanger them directly. Therefore, persuasion is considered the best option.

The immensity of the Middle Eastern crisis has turned the region into an inferno. If Israel implements the UN resolutions by withdrawing to the 1967 borders, then there would be peace. But peace in the Middle East would be a declaration of war on the lucrative heavy arms industry in the US which exports billions of worth of military arsenal to the oil-rich region.

Conclusion

The Muslim countries and especially the Arab allies of the United States have been emphasizing to the Bush Administration that the root-cause of every trouble in their region is the Palestinian catastrophe. At the time when the presidential election campaign is about to kick off, Bush has felt the need to start the 'peace process'. Ariel Sharon is the second Likudian prime minister who has been goaded into a dialogue, which has shown all signs of failure even before starting.

The first Likudian prime minister who was driven into a 'peace process' was Yitzhak Shamir. He admitted that he had gone to the American-sponsored peace conference with the intention of dragging on the so-called peace talks for 'years and years', and to go on encouraging more and more settlements. Ran Ha Cohen calls the Oslo Accords "the great Oslo deceit".[186] The only remnant of those Accords today is the Palestinian Authority that has been badly crippled. Yet, Sharon and Bush are pressurizing the Palestinian Authority to achieve what Sharon with his powerful army, with its US sophisticated arsenal, have badly failed to achieve.

On their part, the Palestinian people ostensibly feel that concealed in the 'road map' is a plan to bring the Palestinian groups in conflict against each other. Colin Powell's visit to the area on 20 June 2003, apart from rubbing shoulders with Sharon, was aimed at throwing stones at close range at the Palestinian militants. According to Powell's apologetic logic pronounced earlier on, it does not matter if Sharon has not actually announced that he accepts the 'road map'. The main broker in the 'peace process' is not prepared to exert pressure on Israel even for uttering specific words for the satisfaction of the other party which has said repeatedly that it accepts the 'road map' unreservedly.

The goodwill expressed by the Palestinian side does not carry the slightest guarantee that the proposed Palestinian State would have sovereignty over its land, sea and air. Under the circumstances, it is the United States that has miles to go to inculcate confidence on the aggrieved side that it is capable of acting impartially, with fairness and equity, to bring a lasting peace in the turbulent region. Until that time, the Palestinians who have suffered a torturous life for the last

Conclusion

fifty-five years, view the position of the US and Israel as two sides of the same coin.

Since the declaration of the American 'road-map', Sharon did not even pretend by words or deeds that he sees himself liable to abide by its terms. He vigorously pursued his aggressive policy of assassinations and then joined the chorus with the Americans for blaming the Palestinians. Almost all the helicopter gunship attacks have cost the lives of innocent bystanders, some of them children. This murdering spree reached its zenith by the end of August 2003. Yet, in early September, it qualified for honours from the Moroccan government, which invited the Israeli Foreign Minister to visit Rabat for talks to promote bilateral relations. At least, the Moroccan authorities should have demanded cessation of extra-judicial killings by Israel in return for improving bilateral relations.

In order to strive for their rights, it is of paramount importance that the Arabs and Muslims articulate a unified strategy and work meticulously towards the common goals. How can they possibly expect to win the respect of others if they have no clear vision of common objectives? Disunity among them is the main impediment to progress. In the new millennium, there is simply no scope for the old ways of totalitarianism, tyrannies, oppression and injustice. If the oppressed Arabs and Muslims are to win their rights, then there is no other alternative than a strategy based on unity of purpose and tolerance, free from extremes.

The radical ideology with its spiteful grudge and malice has rained terror on the Muslim community. Massacre on a mammoth scale has taken place in the city of Najaf in Iraq after the Friday prayers on 29 August 2003. CNN has given more coverage to the tragedy than the government-controlled Arab TV channels. Among the independent Arab satellite networks, *Al-Jazeerah, Al-Arabiya,* and *ANN* have been fair and quite balanced in reporting the event. Other channels, like, *Sahar, Al-Manar* and *Al-Alam* have dedicated themselves on covering the calamity from every conceivable angle. The crime is an affront to the teachings of all the religions. At the time of writing, more than a hundred innocent worshippers are reported to have been killed and over 230 injured.

Conclusion

What type of evil upbringing might it have been which cultivated and injected poisonous hatred in the heart of one human being against another? What type of religious perversion might it have been, which declared people of other Islamic Schools as non-believers, and permitted the shedding of their blood and violation of their honour? The level of bestiality to which these savages are prepared to fall to serve their malicious disposition explains the extent of hatred that has been pumped into their hearts.

The assassination of the leader of the Supreme Council of Islamic Revolution in Iraq, Ayatullah Sayyid Muhammad Baqer Al-Hakim is a declaration of war against the religious personages and religious institutions. It is an act of war against peace. Its aim is to plunge Iraq into a bloody civil war. Who would benefit politically if the Iraqis were to get engaged in fighting each other? This act was treason against Iraq and against the religious morals. There are a number of parties who have been hypersensitive to the mere mention of 'Islamic Revolution'. There are many questions that emerge from the outcome of this horrendous crime that has been executed inside the precincts of Al-Imam Ali mosque, which is revered by millions of Muslims around the world.

Those who have no respect for the sanctity of human life cannot be expected to have any respect for the sanctity of the places of worship. Mosques, churches, monasteries and synagogues have been protected under a clear and specific injunction of the Qur'an and the traditions of the Prophet Muhammad under the Islamic Law. But the rotten ideology of terror recognizes only one law, that which suits its own pathological diversion. If any groups or persons calling themselves Muslims are prepared to issue edicts, permitting violation of the sanctity of human life, then these persons or groups are a source of shame and disgrace to themselves.

In the last 23 years, the bestial Saddam had attempted to assassinate Ayatullah Al-Hakim seven times, killing many members of his noble family, including his eight brothers. A few days before and after his assassination, there have been attempts on the life of other religious authorities. The Americans were warned by Al-Hakim that they have totally failed to protect the sacred places and the lives

Conclusion

of the religious personages. He himself said in his last Friday sermon, minutes before his tragic death, that he had conveyed to the Americans that it is their legal responsibility as occupation forces to provide peace and security in Iraq. But they have been unable to protect even the UN headquarters and foreign embassies in Baghdad. And therefore, he had urged the occupation forces to hand over full charge of security to the Iraqis, who are acquainted with the domestic circumstances. Instead, the occupation forces were insistent at depriving and disarming the guards who had the duty of establishing security in Najaf.

Due to the flagrant negligence of the occupation forces, a car carrying 700 kilograms of explosives safely passed through the security barriers. The resulting ghastly crime did not maim and injure only a few hundred innocent people in the precincts of Al-Imam Ali mosque, but it stabbed the back of millions of peace-loving people around the world. The killers have proved that they are the enemies of God and humanity.

Among the widespread Arab, Islamic and international outrage, King Fahd of Saudi Arabia, the Crown Prince Abdullah and the Defence Minister Prince Sultan issued strongly worded condemnation. The Saudi TV has been televising several programmes after the Riyadh bombing, where the clerics have been reminding about the unequivocal injunctions of the Qur'an and the traditions of the Prophet Muhammad against the killings of innocent people. Although the Saudi authorities have taken measures to contain radicalism at home, it is an undeniable fact that the genie that was nurtured with petrodollars for decades is now out of the bottle.

It is too early to say what is the identity of the suspects who have been arrested. But if these savages, whoever they may be, are capable of committing atrocious crimes on this scale inside Al-Imam Ali mosque, with total disregard for human life, they are quite capable of striking in the heart of Islam's holiest places in Makkah and Madina. Some governments have put all the blame on the shoulders of the Americans. As they are the occupation forces, they have to take a major part of the blame for not stopping the fanatics from crossing the borders and forming new alliance with the

Conclusion

Fidayeen of the devil.

Amidst international outcry, Saddam had the audacity of issuing a statement on an audio, played on *Al-Jazeerah,* denying any involvement in assassinating Al-Hakim. What about the earlier seven attempts on his life? At that time, Saddam had entrenched himself for life on the throne of Iraq, so he was not bothered about the dreadful crimes he was habitually committing with impunity. For the last three decades, first as a Vice President and then as a President, Saddam uprooted the noble pious families of Al-Hakim, Al-Sadr and Bahr-Al-Uloom, and killed many pious and learned personalities. In 1980, he killed the Grand-Ayatullah Muhammad Baqer Al-Sadr, the internationally renowned scholar.

In the wake of the uprising, Saddam attacked the sacred places in Najaf and Karbala in 1991 with helicopters and heavy tanks, and caused widespread damage to the tombs. He got 300,000 people massacred. Thousands of noble souls were buried in mass graves. There are a range of crimes against humanity and against Islam that Saddam has to answer for. If he is innocent, he has nothing to fear. He should be brave enough to come out of hiding and face the charges against him.

All the possibilities have to be investigated about who might have been involved in the cowardly crime of blowing up the people praying in the mosque. The slaughter is the direct result of systematic and categorical attempt for decades to de-Islamize a large section of the Muslim community. The false accusations against those whom they call the 'grave-worshippers' have been forcefully conveyed from the pulpits, even during the pilgrimage season when Muslims of all denominations gather in Makkah. The tapes of the sermons that are available on the market prove this point conclusively. The beliefs and practices of other Muslims have been dishonestly misrepresented. After decades of brain-washing, some ignorant manias in the congregation were bound to take up the cause of killing those Muslims who did not succumb to their thinking.

What needs to be done is to analyze as to who has a history of vicious attacks on mosques and killing of the devotees during Friday prayers? The adherents of this ideology mercilessly killed the

Conclusion

worshippers in Quetta, as they were in a state of prostration in Friday prayers. The cancer has spread with the aid of the petrodollars across Pakistan, Afghanistan, Algeria, Indonesia and other countries. In Pakistan, children in the radically administered religious schools are taught in their curriculum that the Muslims who do not subscribe to their self-righteous beliefs are nonbelievers. This means that intermarriages with them are invalid. Their children are considered illegitimate. Their slaughtered animals cannot be consumed. Their life, property and honour can be violated. When they die, no prayers can be said at their funeral. They cannot be buried in the cemeteries of the Muslims. These are the implications of declaring the opponents unbelievers.

The protagonists of this ideology promoted their poisonous teachings across the Muslim world. This is not a place to give full references of the books that were published on this matter and distributed throughout the Muslim countries. Since the time of Zia-ul-Haq, Pakistan became a fertile ground for the proponents of this ideology. Successive Pakistani governments have tolerated the heads of the organizations that openly advocate and permit the killings of other Muslims. Their websites are a caricature of paranormal hatred they preach against those Muslims whom they see as their rivals. Some of them sit in the National Assembly.

As a direct consequence of such pernicious teachings, there is a history of criminal aggression on the sanctity of the tomb of Al-Imam Ali in Najaf. There is a history of a series of assaults dating back to 1800s on Najaf and Karbala from across the borders. There is a history of mass massacres carried out around the tombs of Al-Imam Ali and Al-Imam Al-Hussain. For different reasons, there is also a history of Saddam's butchery in Najaf and Karbala during his satanic reign. At the time of the popular uprising in 1991, the fiend had given charge of desecrating the sacred places to his son-in-law, Hussein Kamel. The tombs were badly damaged with heavy artillery firing whilst tracking the revolutionaries. But within five years, Hussein Kamel himself was killed by Saddam for treason and his dead body was dragged in the streets.

The challenges facing the Muslim community are draconian

Conclusion

simply because the terror gangsters carry Muslim names. In as much as the radical Zion-neoconservatives have pushed the US into the destructive wars, the genie that has misused the name of Islam, has spread destruction by violating every religious and moral principles. In as much as George W. Bush would eventually realize that the hawkish policies have done more damage than good to the interests of America, the Muslims too would realize that the quagmire of fanatical terrorism has damaged the reputation of the entire community. In as much as Sharon would have to convince himself that his apartheid wall is an anathema to the civilized values, the Muslim extremists, and they are in minority, would have to accede that their onslaught on human life is sacrilegious to the teachings of the Qur'an and the traditions of the Prophet Muhammad. In as much as the role of religion in human society is to promote love, peace and fraternity, the disrespect for human life is an antithesis of religion. In as much as the noble souls who dedicate themselves selflessly for the good of humankind are remembered for their sacrifices, the wicked ones who play havoc with the life of innocent people can only be remembered as anarchists and nihilists. The struggle between good and evil goes on.

References

[1] Scott Thompson, "Michael Ledeen Demands 'Regime Change' in Iran", *Executive Intelligence Review*, 11 July 2003. www.larouchepub.com/other/2003/3027ledeen_iran.html.
[2] Ibid.
[3] Charley Reese, "A Rousing Good Book", *King Features Syndicate*, 21 May 2003. http://rease.king-online.com.
[4] Dr Francis Macnab, "Ordinary Magic – Good Outcomes in spite of Bleak Prospects". www.stmichaels.org.au/services_archive/
[5] "CTBT – A Psychological Profile", www.friends.org.pk/Nuclear.htm.
[6] Eyad El Sarraj, "The Mideast road map is pointless without guiding principles", *The Globe and Mail*, 29 May 2003. www.globeandmail.com.
[7] Joe MacAnthony, "Even the dead do battle in the land of hate", *Sunday Independent*, 12 August 2001.
[8] "No weapons in Iraq? We'll find them in Iran", *Sunday Herald*, 1 June 2003. www.sundayherald.com/
[9] "20 Lies About the War", *The Independent*, 13 July 2003.
[10] http://news.bbc.co.uk/1/hi/programmes/panorama/3032185.stm.
[11] William O. Beeman, "Michael Ledeen: Neoconservative Guru", *The Daily Star*, Beirut, 9 May 2003.
[12] Scott Thompson, "Michael Ledeen Demands 'Regime Change' in Iran", *Executive Intelligence Review*, 11 July 2003.
[13] www.sundayherald.com/, 1 June 2003.
[14] Eric Hobsbawm, "America's imperial delusion", *The Guardian*, 14 June 2003.
[15] Jim Lobe, "An Iraqi 'quackmire' in the making", *Asia Times Online*, 24 June 2003. www.atimes.com/atimes/Middle_East/
[16] Robert Fisk, "The troops are afraid to go out at night", *The Independent*, 31 May 2003.
[17] "Halliburton doubles price tag for Iraq oil work", *Toronto Star*, 14 June 2003. www.thestar.com.
[18] Carola Hoyos, "Oil groups snub US on Iraq deals", *FT.com Financial Times*, 24 July 2003.
[19] "U.S. Banks Vying for Work Renewing Iraqi Finance System", *Quicken Home*, 12 June 2003.
[20] David Scheffer, "Comment: A legal minefield for Iraq's occupiers", *Financial Times*, 24 July 2003.
[21] www.californiapeaceaction.org/campaigns/rumsfeld/threads.htm

References

[22] Jeremy Scahill, "The Saddam in Rumsfeld's Closet", *Common Dreams News Centre*, 26 June 2003. First published in *CommonDreams.org*, 2 August 2002.
[23] Geoffrey Holland, "The US supplied anthrax to Iraq", *The Badger*, May 2003. www.paulflynnmp.co.uk.
[24] Simon Robinson, "Grounding Planes the Wrong Way", *Time*, Vol. 162, No. 2, 14 July 2003.
[25] Paul Krugman, "Who's Accountable", *New York Times*, 10 June 2003.
[26] Rupert Cornwell, "CIA deliberately misled UN arms inspector, says senator", *Independent.co.uk*, 18 June 2003.
[27] Nicholas D. Kristoff, "White House in Denial", *New York Times*, 13 June 2003.
[28] James Risen and Douglas Jehl, "Expert Said To Tell Legislators He Was Pressed to Distort Some Evidence", *Common Dreams News Centre*, 26 June 2003. First published in *New York Times*, 25 June 2003.
[29] Thomas Shanker and Eric Schmitt, "A Nation At War: Strategic Shift; Pentagon Expects Long-Term Access to Key Iraq Bases", *The New York Times*, 20 April 2003.
[30] Charley Reese, "Is It Important", *King Features Syndicate*, 11 June 2003. http://reese.king-online.com.
[31] Giles Tremlitt, "Troops Bear 'Moor Killer' Badges. *The Guardian*, 25 July 2003.
[32] "Iraq Survey shows ' Humanitarian Emergency' ", *UNICEF*, 8 Dec. 1999.
[33] Leslie C. Green, "War Crimes, Crimes against Humanity, and Command Responsibility", USA: *Naval War College Review*, 1997, p. 3.
[34] Derrik Mercer (ed.), *Chronicle of the 20th Century*, Paris: Jacques Legrand, and London: Chronicle Communications, 1988, p. 631.
[35] Ibid., p. 630.
[36] "CTBT- A Psychological Profile", www.friends.org.pk/Nuclear.htm.
[37] Ian Brownie (ed.), *Basic Documents on Human Rights*, Oxford, UK: Clarendon Press, 1971, p. 93.
[38] Ibid., p. 94.
[39] "Experts at U.S. Conference on global warming say Bush's position 'ludicrous' ", *News Canada.com*, 25 July 2003.
[40] Kevin Bales, *Disposable People New Slavery in the Global Economy*, California, USA: University of California Press, 1999, pp. 100 & 192.
[41] Ibid., pp. 16-17.

References

[42] "Children in Poverty America's Ongoing War", *Hearts & Minds*, www.heartsandminds.org/articles/childpov.htm.
[43] Emma Williams, "The reck injustice", *The Spectator*, 17 May 2003. www.spectator.co.uk/
[44] Ibid.
[45] "Has your country ratified", *International Labour Organization*, www.ilo.org/public/english/standards/ipec/index.htm.
[46] "World Day against Child Labour 12 June 2003", *International Labour Organization*.
[47] International Programme on the Elimination of Child Labour (IPEC), *Wounded Childhood*, Switzerland: International Labour Organization, 2003, p. vii.
[48] Ibid.
[49] Bales, *Disposable People*, 1999, p.237, quoting from "Migrant Bonded Labour", *Incidence of Bonded Labour in India*, vol.3.
[50] Ibid., p.237.
[51] Ibid., pp. 196-197.
[52] Ibid., pp. 3-4.
[53] Ibid., p. 5.
[54] Ibid., pp. 196-197 and p. 203.
[55] Judith Ennew, *Exploitation of Children*, East Sussex, UK: Wayland (Publishers) Ltd., 1996.
[56] Jonathan Sivners, "Child Labour in Pakistan", *The Atlantic online*. www.educationplanet.com.
[57] Adel Safty, *From Camp David to the Gulf*, New York and Montreal: Black Rose Books, 1992, p. 178, quoted from Colman McCarthy, "Israeli Justice", *The Washington Post*, reproduced in the *Guardian Weekly*, 22 July 1990.
[58] Michael Palumbo, *Imperial Israel*, London: Bloomsbury Publishing, 1990, p. 234.
[59] Ibid., pp. 237-238.
[60] Ibid., p. 239.
[61] David McDowall, *The Palestinians The Road to Nationhood*, London: Minority Rights Publications, 1994, p. 136.
[62] Ibid., p. 136, quoted from Ramsden and Shenker, *Learning the Hard Way*, p. 17.
[63] Sophie Goodchild and Jo Dillon, "The scandal of Britain's asylum children", *The Independent*, 15 June 2003.

References

[64] "Post-Crisis Recovery and the Obstacles of Landmines", *UNDP and Mine Action,* 17 August 2001.
[65] "Landmines Campaign Condemns Recent Mine Use", *ICBL*, http://www.icbl.org.
[66] Edward Lawson, *Encyclopedia of Human Rights,* London and Pennsylvania: Taylor & Francis, 1991, p. 100.
[67] David Usborne, "Global accord on small arms trade sabotaged by US", *The Independent,* 25 July 2001.
[68] Martin Gilbert, *A History of the Twentieth Century, Vol.3, 1952-1999,* London: HarperCollins Publishers, 1999, p. 391.
[69] "CTBT – A Psychological Profile", www.friends.org.pk/Nuclear.htm.
[70] Ibid.
[71] Gilbert, *A history of the Twentieth Century, Vol 3,* 1999, p. 637.
[72] Ibid., p. 638.
[73] Ibid., p. 737.
[74] Ibid., p. 828.
[75] Ibid., p. 829.
[76] "A Short History of the Human Rights Movement", www.hrweb.org.
[77] James Avery Joyce, *The New Politics of Human Rights,* London: The Macmillan Press, 1978, p. 83.
[78] http://www.ariga.com/humanrights/
[79] Palumbo, *Imperial Israel,* 1990, p. 10.
[80] "Israel and Torture", *The Sunday Times,* 19 June 1977.
[81] Joyce, *The New Politics of Human Rights,* 1978, p. 137.
[82] Ibid., p. 138.
[83] Ibid., pp. 269-270.
[84] Ibid., p. 272.
[85] Lawson, *Encyclopedia of Human Rights,* 1991, p. 1378.
[86] Ibid., p. 1225.
[87] Law Soceity, "Extra Judicial Execution in Balat Refugee Camp", 23 May 2003. www.jerusalem.indymedia.org/
[88] "Human Rights Monitors Needed in Israel-Palestinian Conflict", *Human Rights Watch,* 6 July 2001. www.hrw.org/Press/
[89] Green, "War Crimes, 1997, p. 1.
[90] Ibid., p. 9.
[91] Ibid., p. 12.
[92] Robert Fisk, "When Journalists refuse to tell the truth about Israel", *The Independent,* 17 April, 2001.

References

[93] http://news.bbc.co.uk/hi/english/audiovideo/programmes/panorama/
[94] CAIR-NET, "Muslims Protest Sharon White House", 25 June 2001. http://www.cair-net.org.
[95] "Rumsfeld Wrong to Attack Belgian Human Rights Law", *Common Dreams Progressive Newswire*, 26 June 2003. www.Commondreams.org.
[96] Green, "War Crimes", 1997, pp. 21-22.
[97] Evlyn Leopold, "U.S. Rapped for Campaign Against New Global Court", *Reuters*, 12 June 2003.
[98] Ian Traynor, "US plays aid card to fix war crimes exemption", *The Guardian*, 12 June 2003.
[99] Ibid., p. 123.
[100] Gilbert, *A History, vol. 3*, 1999, pp. 826-827.
[101] *Human Rights Annual Report 2000*, London: Foreign & Commonwealth Office, p.53.
[102] Mercer (ed.), *Chronicle*, 1988, p. 57.
[103] Green, "War Crimes", *Naval*, 1997, p. 2.
[104] Ibid., p. 4.
[105] Ibid., p. 7.
[106] Ibid., p. 3.
[107] Ibid., p. 20.
[108] David Rieff, *Slaughterhouse Bosnia and the failure of the West*, UK: Vintage, 1995, p. 26.
[109] Jenine di Giovanni, "Men who pulled trigger are ones we want tried", *The Times*, 3 July 2001.
[110] David Rohde, *Endgame: The Betrayal and Fall of Srebrenica, Europe's Worst Massacre since World War II*, New York: Farrar, Straus and Giroux, 1997.
[111] David Rohde, "A Cautionary Tale for US Before it enters Bosnia", *The Christian Science Monitor*, 13 October 1995.
[112] David Rohde, "Bosnian Serbs Poisoned Streams to capture Refugees, Muslims say", *The Christian Science Monitor*, 24 October 1995.
[113] http://www.haverford.edu/rlg/sells/rape.html.
[114] Robert Fisk, "Our shame over Srebrenica", *The Independent*, 12 July 2001.
[115] Gilbert, *A History, vol. 3*, 1999, p. 825.
[116] *The Times Magazine*, 14 April 2001.
[117] Mohamed Khodr, "Bush's Hail to the Chief Putin", *Media Monitors Network*, 25 June 2001.

References

[118] "This war cannot succeed - The killing will not subdue Chechnya", *The Guardian*, 24 January, 2001.

[119] Patrick Cockburn, "Terrorising journalists to hide a brutal truth", *The Independent*, 11 August 2001.

[120] Larry C. Johnson, *The New York Times*, 10 July 2001.

[121] Charley Reese, "Missile-defence plan could backfire on US", *OrlandoSentinel.com*, 14 June 2001.

[122] *The Independent*, 26 July 2001.

[123] Michael McCarthy et al., *The Independent*, 12 July 2001.

[124] Gilbert, *A History of the Twentieth Century, Volume 2, 1933-1951*, London: HarperCollins Publishers, 1998, p. 407.

[125] Ian Gurney, "Next stop Iran?", *Online Journal*, 21 July 2003. www.onlinejournal.com/Commentary/072103Gurney/

[126] Marianne Brun-Rovet and Edward Alden, "September 11 report raises Saudi question", *FT.Com, Financial Times,* 25 July 2003.

[127] Joel Skousen, "Analysis of White House Obstruction of 911 investigation", *World Affairs Brief,* c. 2003, JoelSkousen.com.

[128] Yasmin Alibhai-Brown, "Britain must distance itself from America", *Daily Times,* 21 June 2003.

[129] Patrick J. Buchanan, "Whose War?", *The American Conservative,* 24 March 2003.

[130] Phyllis Bennis, "Going Global: Building a Movement Against Empire", *Foreign Policy in Focus,* May 2003. www.fpig.org.

[131] Christopher Hoskins, "Blair has to make America return the favour", *Financial Times,* 26 March 2003.

[132] Brian Whitaker, "US thinktanks give lessons in foreign policy", *Guardian Unlimited,* 19 August 2002. www.guardian.co.uk.

[133] Michael A. Ledeen, "Political Attack Can Remove Terror Masters in Syria and Iran", 30 April 2003. http://www.aei.org/news/

[134] Michael A. Ledeen, "How We Could Lose", *National Review Online,* 9 January 2003.

[135] Brian Whitaker, "Conflict and catchphrases", *Guardian Unlimited,* 24 February 2003. www.guardian.co.uk.

[136] Michael A. Ledeen, "Unnoticed Bombshell", *National Review Online,* 11 February 2002.

[137] Michael A. Ledeen, "The Revolution Continues", *Nation Review Online,* 25 March 2002.

[138] Robert Fisk, "Saddam or No Saddam, Iraqi Press Will Always Have Censors", *The Independent,* 12 June 2003.

References

[139] Edward W. Said, *Peace & its Discontents*, London: Vintage, 1995, p. 157.
[140] Ibid., p. 158.
[141] "Interfaith Alliance Opposes Daniel Pipes Nomination", www.cair-net.org. 21 July 2003.
[142] Ibid.
[143] Daniel Gillespie, "Middle East Analyst Calls for Speedy US Withdrawal From Iraq", *CNSNews.com*, 25 July 2003.
[144] Steve Brown, " 'Militant Islam' Critic Faces Tough Fight for Spot on Peace Institute", *CNSNews.com*, 23 April 2003.
[145] *Jerusalem Post*, 24 July 2003.
[146] Fiachra Gibbons, "US 'is an empire in denial' ", *The Guardian*, 2 June 2003.
[147] http://www.msnbc.com/news/659057.asp?cp1=1.
[148] Richard Bernstein, "Experts on Islam Pointing Fingers at One Another", *The New York Times*, 3 November 2001.
[149] http://www.nytimes.com/2001/11/03/arts/03EXPE.html.
[150] http://www.worldaffairsforum.org/calendar.htm.
[151] "Jewish groups and some conservatives have been lobbying the president to stop courting certain Muslim leaders" *Washington Post*, 18 November 2001.
[152] *Jerusalem Post*, 24 July 2002.
[153] Janine di Giovanni, *The Times*, 16 April 2002.
[154] Paul de Rooij, "Amnesty International & Israel: Say it isn't so!" *CounterPunch*, 31 October 2002. www.counterpunch.org/rooij1031.html.
[155] *Reuters*, 13 June 2002.
[156] CAIR-NET, 13 June 2002. http://www.cair-net.org.
[157] Suzanne Goldenberg et al., "Sharon hails raid as great success", *The Guardian*, 24 July 2002.
[158] Charley Reese, "Tragic Conflict", *King Features Syndicate*, 16 June 2003. http://reese.king-online.com.
[159] Edward Epstein, "Pelosi supports Israel's attacks on Hamas Demos slam Bush for criticizing strikes", *San Francisco Chronicle*, 14 June 2003.
[160] Oona King, "Israel can halt this now", *The Guardian*, 12 June 2003.
[161] Charley Reese, "Only thing to negotiate is timetable for Israel's withdrawal", *OrlandoSentinel.com*, 21 June 2001.
[162] http://electronicintifada.net/v2/article1284.shtml.

References

[163] Junaid Alam, "The Wolf Who Cried Wolf: Charging Anti-Semitism and Extending the Iron Wall", *CounterPunch*, 26 October 2002.

[164] CAIR-NET, 25 July 2002. http://www.cair-net.org.

[165] Shlomi Segall, "Why I won't serve Sharon", *The Guardian*, 5 July 2002.

[166] Michael A. Hoffman II, "The 'Road Map' for Peace is a Swindle", *The Hoffman Wire*, 3 June 2003, www.hoffman-info.com/wire6.html.

[167] John Bagot Glubb, *Peace in the Holy Land,* London: Hodder and Stoughton, 1971, p. 364.

[168] Ibid., p. 365.

[169] Ibid., p 367.

[170] Nur Masalha, *A Land Without a People*, London: Faber & Faber, 1997, p. 97.

[171] Charley Reese, "Bad Idea", *King Features Syndicate,* 2 June 2003, http://reese.king-online.com.

[172] Michael Palumbo, *The Palestinian Catastrophe,* London and Boston: Faber & Faber, 1987, p. 210.

[173] Ibid., p. 211, quoted from *Koteret Rashit,* 27 February 1985.

[174] Ibid., p. 212.

[175] Ibid. pp. 212-213.

[176] McDowall, *The Palestinians*, 1994, p. 76.

[177] Ibid., p. 77.

[178] Edward Said, "Freud, Zionism and Vienna", *Al-Ahram weekly online.* http://www.ahram.org.eg/weekly/2001/525/op2.htm.

[179] Nicholas Davies, *The Unknown Maxwell,* London: Sidgwick & Jackson, 1993, p. 292.

[180] Ibid., p. 291.

[181] Tom Bower, *Maxwell The Final Verdict,* London: HarperCollins Publishers, 1995, pp. 263-264.

[182] Davies, *The Unknown Maxwell,* 1993, p. 298.

[183] Ibid., p. 297.

[184] Ibid., p. 296.

[185] Palumbo, The Palestinian, 1987, p. 142.

[186] Ran Ha Cohen, "The Apartheid Wall", www.antiwar.com.